NICOLA MORGAN
The Teenage Guide to

WALKER BOOKS
AND SUBSIDIARIES

LONDON · BOSTON · SYDNEY · AUCKLAND

Contents

SECTION THREE

Dealing With and Preventing Symptoms of Stress

Conclusion

APPENDIX

Resources

Introduction

When I tell adults about this book, most think it's a good idea. But a few say things like, "*We* survived without a book to help us. Why can't today's teenagers just get on with it? They'll survive." I have no sympathy with that view!

Here's why.

First, just because there was nothing to help us "in our day" doesn't mean that was better. If there'd been a sympathetic and informative book when I was a teenager, I'd have used it, and I bet most people would.

Second, why be satisfied with just *surviving*? Isn't it better to *thrive* and achieve your potential instead?

Third, although a bit of stress doesn't usually lead to illness or serious consequences, sometimes it does. And too much stress over a long time often makes us ill and unable to do our best. If we can prevent that, surely we should try?

Importantly, if you learn how to manage stress while you're young, you can use the same skills throughout your life. That will save heartache, illness and money.

Another thing some people say is, "In my day we didn't even have 'stress' – it's a modern invention." I agree that we *talk* about stress more nowadays, because we know more about it, but stress itself isn't new. And nor is the word – back in 1904, the sociologist G. Stanley Hall described adolescence as a period of "upheaval and trauma, storm and stress". In past generations, people who became ill with what we now know are symptoms of stress might have been given addictive tranquillisers, or left to become more ill, or ended up in a mental hospital for a while, or even for a long time. There were dramatic and unpleasant medical remedies; anything except good, healthy, sympathetic ways to prevent stress causing trouble.

It's far better to learn to manage stress *before* it causes bad symptoms and spoils this period of your life, surely?

It's important to realize that not all stress is bad, though. Feeling nervous before an exam or an interview can help us perform extra well. Worrying about a decision can help us think it through properly. And having some difficult days or periods can help us appreciate holidays and breaks even more. But when stress goes on for too long and is too strong, when it gets in the way of happiness and achievement and health and stops us doing what we want and need to do, that is not good.

Teenagers also have many stresses which we didn't have in our day. The pressure of exams is greater and more constant; the price of failure or misbehaviour can be higher; risks and temptations are often stronger. Adults may have forgotten other things that make adolescence difficult: changing bodies, fear of the future, new knowledge about the sometimes-scary things in the wider world.

You may be going through problems that your parents either didn't have or have forgotten. You may be worried about your friends. You may have had bad experiences with social media. You may be experiencing bullying. You may feel sad or scared or angry or confused in ways you find hard to talk about. This book is here to help. And there are many resources at the end to help you further.

So, the advice in this book aims to help you worry less about whatever you worry about and to give you strategies for relaxation. I'm going to help you recognise and manage stress before it becomes too difficult. And throughout the book there are real comments from real people – teenagers and adults – who share their memories and advice to show you that you are not alone.

The Teenage Guide to Stress will make everything feel more normal, less stressful, less worrying, more positive. It will help you not just survive but also thrive. Being a teenager does not have to be so hard.

Nicola Morgan
Edinburgh, 2013
www.nicolamorgan.com

How the Book Works

SECTION ONE explains what stress is and what it can do to you and looks at some of the ways in which teenage stresses may be different from others.

SECTION TWO deals with loads of issues that worry many teenagers and offers guidance, sympathy and advice. For many of you, simply discovering that your worries are normal will be enough to make you feel better. Understanding will get you a long way.

I'll also talk about some pre-existing conditions you may have, such as OCD or dyslexia, and how they might be different during adolescence. If you're worrying about something that isn't mentioned, this does not mean you are the only person in the world with that problem. You're not. It just means this book isn't long enough to mention every human worry.

SECTION THREE looks at ways of dealing with and preventing symptoms of stress, as well as healthy ways of looking after your mind and body. And once you've learnt what to do, I suggest you teach those skills to the adults you know. If you have a stressed adult in your life, that's probably making your life tougher, too, so it makes sense for everyone to understand how to deal with stress. Adults don't know it all.

At the end of the book, there are lists of resources for all the topics I cover.

What is a "trusted adult?"

Often, part of my advice is to talk to a "trusted adult". But what do I mean and how do you find one? Many adults want to help you, even if they don't personally know you, and many have special training in different aspects of adolescence or stress or various problems. The best person to choose will depend on you, your particular situation and the adults in your life. Never think that there is no one for you – I promise there is, but you may have to go and find them.

In an ideal world, parents or carers would be the first and best people to talk to. But it's not an ideal world. You may not have a parent or carer, or they may be wrapped up in their own problems, which may not be their fault. (Parents are human and no one is perfect.) You may have a bad relationship with them. Some may have problems with alcohol or drugs or mental illness and not be in a position to help. Some parents, unfortunately, are not "trusted adults". Sometimes, even if you do have a good relationship with them and they are wonderful people, you still may not feel able to talk to them about a particular problem.

So, if you can't talk to your parents for any reason, who

else could you talk to? Depending on your particular situation and worry, here are some suggestions. All the professionals on this list – teachers, doctors and health workers etc – have a duty to protect you. This means that if they believe that you or another person are in danger of abuse, harm or neglect, they have a duty to inform a relevant adult, but they will discuss it with you first. They will talk to you about which adults will be the best people to tell, focusing on what is best for you. They are also not allowed to cover up a serious crime – no one is.

- **A teacher you like.** Teachers are not always trained in dealing with every problem but all have some training in what to do when a student comes to them for help. They know how to reassure you and make sure you find the right help.

- **Your head of year**, year tutor, "guidance" teacher or whatever name your school gives to the teacher in charge of "pastoral care" or wellbeing. (If you don't know who it is, ask.) These teachers have training in dealing with confidential problems.

- **Your GP.** Doctors must keep everything confidential. However, as for all professionals, if they believe you are in serious danger, they must act to protect you, which might mean informing another adult after discussion with you.

- **Childline.** This is the best-known organisation for helping young people and is hugely respected and trusted. They have heard everything and know exactly what to say to help you. You can phone or have an online chat; phone calls are free and won't appear on the bill. They guarantee 100% confidentiality and will only take action if they believe your life is in immediate danger. Their website tells you a lot about the process of getting help. Take a look now, so you know what's there if you need it.
- **Any doctor or member of staff at a health clinic for young people.** Do an internet search on the phrase "health clinic for young people [enter name of your town or postcode]". They know how to help you in any medical or mental-health situation; advice is free and confidential (as with GP consultations); and you can make the appointment yourself, without being registered in advance.
- **A youth worker attached to Social Services**, if you happen to know one or have met one through a youth group, for example.
- **Any adult you've known for long enough to know they are trustworthy**, for example a family friend, relative, or the parent of a friend. For a general reassuring chat, they can be fantastic

and all you need. But for more serious or specific problems, such as anorexia, self-harm, depression and anything involving medicine, mental health or the law, speak to someone who has had relevant training.

- **Any helpline aimed at young people suffering from a particular problem.** Use the internet or my resource list at the back of this book to find a relevant organisation. See if it has a helpline and phone it. Such organisations often have online chat lines, too, so that you don't need to speak to anyone in person.

BE CAREFUL

Sometimes it is hard to know who to trust. It's important to follow your instincts, stay aware and alert, and to remember that not everyone is good. Some people are bad and are clever at making you trust them. The safest thing, if you are in any doubt at all, is to go through your school guidance department or to phone Childline.

Chat rooms may be good places to talk to others suffering from your problem but they are not places where you should necessarily trust people. Never give any personal details in a chat room, even your name or the school you go to. Never arrange to meet someone on your own. And if you ever feel slightly uncomfortable, even a tiny bit worried, tell a proper "trusted adult" and see what they say. Some dangerous adults hang around chat rooms pretending to be teenagers, and are very clever at befriending vulnerable people.

When choosing websites or chat rooms about a particular problem, be very cautious, selecting those with good medical advice and adult supervision.

Even the people on my list above are not necessarily perfect. Clever bad people can sometimes get through all the checks. So, my final advice when thinking about who will be your trusted adult is this: don't just speak to one. Choose two, separately.

That way, I believe you will be as safe as possible and your two trusted adults can really help you.

Why should you trust me?

I have done my very best to give good advice in this book. I've worked hard and spoken to lots of people. However, I simply can't know every situation and I can't see into your mind or home or fully understand everything that is going on for you so that I can make everything right. Also, sometimes a situation is extra complicated and advice from one book won't be enough.

If you have medical worries, it's important to see a medical expert. I am not qualified to give medical advice and no advice in this book can replace professional help for serious medical conditions. I hope it will direct you to the right help where necessary.

How scientific is this book? Well, for a start, it's not a science book; it's a self-help book. But it's based on my understanding and experience and the things I believe and have discovered, or which I think are worth trying. Occasionally I mention research, but I don't give references as I would if this were an academic book. And I deliberately only mention research that I believe to be good or interesting, and which is reported in a high-quality journal.

Also, I've consulted many experts in many different areas. This book is not just the advice of one person, but is informed by the views of many experts and people who care very much that you should be as healthy, happy and successful as possible. You might sometimes not realize just how much we care.

17

A note about "he or she"

It's annoying saying "he or she" so I'll usually just choose one or the other, randomly. In almost every case it makes no difference: boys and girls have most of the same stresses, though they may react somewhat differently to them. Boys sometimes hide their feelings more and some are brought up to think that being emotional is wrong, but they still have those feelings of hurt or sadness or anger inside. So, understand that when I say one or the other, I usually mean both.

SECTION ONE

The What and Why of Stress for Teenagers

What is Stress?

We react to danger, fear or any need for sudden action with what is called the "fight or flight" response. When we're threatened by something dangerous, our brain instantly triggers the release of a range of chemicals that make our bodies quickly respond. Two of the chemicals are adrenalin and cortisol. Between them, they have various effects including: your heart pumps blood more quickly, your muscles get more oxygen, your skin goes cold because more blood has gone to muscles and organs, your pupils expand to let in more light, and you stop focusing on tiny and irrelevant details and concentrate on the main danger.

Let me give you an example of how this worked for me: there's the little-known story of the time I jumped over a really high gate. Under normal circumstances, I couldn't have done this. However, at the time I was being chased by a vicious goose – don't laugh – and badly needed to jump that gate. Fortunately, my "fight or flight" mechanism kicked in and my body was flooded with instant strength and bravery (well, maybe not bravery). I wisely used the strength for "flight".

This reaction is healthy, though I wouldn't have said that if I'd broken my arm falling over the gate. But if stress keeps repeating itself over too long a time, you are constantly in the "fight or flight" mode, with nothing to fight or to run from. This tends to happen with many modern stresses: there isn't a real danger, so the danger doesn't noticeably pass, which means you don't get rid of the stress chemicals. Cortisol can then build up and affect your health negatively in many different ways. An important example is that it can harm your immune system so that you get more illnesses.

You need a balance of stress and relaxation in your life. After a stressful thing, you need something to relax you and get rid of the cortisol.

So, when I talk about "feeling stressed", I'm not saying it's necessarily a bad thing and I'm not going to try to remove all the stress from your lives. What I want to do is show you how to remove unnecessary stress – particularly constant worry or unnecessary panic – and learn to manage it, controlling it for yourselves, recognising neg-ative symptoms and learning to deal with them.

20

Resilience

People talk a lot about the importance of developing "resilience" nowadays. Resilience is the ability to bounce back after something bad or difficult. Some people believe it's one of the most important life-skills. Psychologists say that, although people are born with different levels of resilience or acquire it through early childhood, it can also be learnt and practised later. This book aims to make you more resilient, first by tackling your worries and putting them in context, and second by offering strategies for dealing with stress.

Resilience will make you strong. It will help you thrive on positive stress and avoid negative stress. You can't prevent bad things happening but you can do something about how you deal with them. You can learn to come back stronger.

"When life knocks you down, keep getting up.
Believe in yourself, even if everyone else around
you does not. Believe you can do better, be better.
Don't allow others to set your limits."
Malorie Blackman, author

What are the Symptoms of Stress?

Sometimes the symptoms are obvious. You feel nervous, panicky, constantly worried, and find it hard to sleep. You may find it hard to concentrate because you are actively fretting about something. You don't need me to tell you that you're stressed in these situations!

But, very often, you may have symptoms you don't realize are caused by stress. You might not realize that it's causing your headaches, stomach aches or dizzy spells. It's common for people of any age to worry about headaches, for instance, and think they must be caused by a serious illness. Check your symptoms with a doctor first, of course, but once they've reassured you that nothing serious is going on, you can focus on the advice in this book.

So, here are symptoms often caused by stress:

- A feeling of tightness high in your chest
- Feeling that you can't take a full breath in
- Persistent headaches (including migraines) and stomach aches
- Difficulty sleeping – either difficulty getting to sleep, or waking in the middle of the night and not being able to get back to sleep
- Negative thoughts that won't go away
- Loss of appetite
- Biting finger-nails (or any other bits of you!)

- Mood swings
- Feeling anxious and panicky
- Not being able to concentrate

All these symptoms are common. But no one wants to put up with stuff like this too often or for too long. All these things can prevent you from performing at your best and being happy. If you suffer from these symptoms and your doctor has reassured you that you are not ill, you will benefit from some of the strategies in SECTION THREE.

"Learn to recognise when you are stressed and find ways to keep yourself calm and grounded. Make time to do something you enjoy every day." **Dani, adult**

Is Stress Different for Teenagers?

Of course, adults have stressful things to deal with too. But there are special challenges in adolescence and many people agree that being a teenager is often extra stressful. I can't say if it's more or less stressful than being an adult, but I can say that it's different and that adults sometimes don't appreciate how difficult it can be and why.

Two separate sets of pressures make you different from children and adults. I call them **Stage of Life** and **State of Brain**.

Stage of Life

Here are some problems that tend to affect teenagers more than younger children and adults:

- ○ **Exams.** Teenagers generally face more important exams than either children or adults. The pressures, and worrying about failure, can be huge. Choosing the subjects for those exams often feels as though you are making life-changing decisions.
- ○ **Greater knowledge of the world.** You can't be shielded from everything as you were when younger but you may not be able to put things into perspective as an adult should. Frightening things can get out of proportion and take over your mind.
- ○ **Pressure to conform** to images of perfection and celebrity success. You are faced with impossible images of perfection (usually artificial) and may not realize that real people are not like that.
- ○ **Pressure to impress your friends.** It's well known that teenagers care a lot about what their friends think and find it hard to ignore.
- ○ **Your changing body.** You may not like how quickly (or slowly!) your body is changing. You may

24

develop a distorted view of how you look to other people.

- **Fear of the future.** As a child you were able to live in a kind of dream world where anything seemed possible, but now you may start to worry about practical things like jobs and money. When you were younger, adults could tell you not to worry but they can't reassure you so easily now.

- **Dealing with sad things in your or your friends' lives.** Again, it's hard to protect teenagers from such realities. If you have to deal with a friend being ill or depressed or going through a terrible time, this can affect you deeply. You may also have to deal with the death of a friend or loved one; of course, this can happen at any age, but children tend to be cared for and protected by an adult and adults tend to have their own support systems, as well as a more developed brain and greater life experience.

- **The dangers and problems of social media.** Some teenagers are horrendously affected by online bullying or by making an innocent mistake which they have to pay a heavy price for.

- **Hormones.** We all have hormones but the new rushes of male or female hormones in adolescence can hugely affect mood. For some teenage girls, PMS (pre-menstrual syndrome) is particularly difficult.

"If you don't have regrets about your teenage years, you didn't do it right. In fact, you're not doing it right unless it feels all wrong." **Anne, adult**

"I was the teacher's pet; the strong person with an answer for everything. But it wasn't all plain sailing. Looking back I realize how much of a brave face I put on things; especially those I found distressing. It's only now as an adult I wish I'd been astute enough to recognise the depth of my problems. [...] When things really started to fall apart for me in sixth form, I became the difficult pupil ... but no one asked why and I wouldn't say I received any positive interventions. I wish ... we'd had general emotional wellbeing education and discussions in class to help destigmatise mental health issues." **Katie Wilson**

Young judge of the Children and Young People's Mental Health Coalition's "Resilience and Results" competition

"When my bunch were young teenagers, we were more concerned with surviving each day at school and our social position. Lately we have become more aware of the immediate future (e.g. uni) and I reckon

that later on we will start to worry about the
bigger picture of the future." **Jenni, 17**

———

"I don't really worry, due to how unpredictable the
future is. [...] I may have this mindset from having
family stories like a relative who went to university
for architecture, switched to a degree in physical
education, became a PE teacher for a while and
then set up a production company, produced their
own sketch show and is now an actor/producer."
Patrick, 18

———

State of Brain

The teenage brain works differently from both children's brains and adult brains. (My book *Blame My Brain* covers this in detail.) These brain differences can explain many things you find stressful.

The physical changes start well before your thirteenth birthday. Roughly from age ten or eleven to eleven or twelve, your brain produces many more connections between neurons. Then, roughly from age thirteen, much of the extra volume is pruned away, leaving stronger, better connections. From then on, your brain focuses on strengthening the networks of connections, as you become more expert in the things you are good at. When you don't spend time on a particular activity, you will lose some of that ability (though you can get it back later if you try).

Here are some of the stress-related things that can be explained by differences in the teenage brain:

- **Finding it hard to control your emotions.** We know that the teenage emotional systems are very well developed but a part of your brain called the prefrontal cortex (which enables you to control emotions and make good decisions) is not fully developed until the mid twenties.

- **Taking "bad" risks**, especially when your friends or peer group are involved. The part of the brain you need to make good decisions is that underdeveloped prefrontal cortex. And the parts that make you want to do something exciting or risky are in your very well-developed emotional centres. There's also evidence that the brain's reward systems in some teenagers make them react differently to the desire to take risks. And teenagers take slightly longer deciding whether something is risky. All this helps explain why some teenagers make bad decisions about risk.

- **Being extra embarrassed about things** that adults don't find so embarrassing. We know that

28

teenagers (perhaps particularly girls) use their brains differently when thinking about embarrassing social situations. Scientists have seen this difference using brain-imaging machines.

- **Sleep problems.** Adolescent sleep patterns are biologically different. You actually need more sleep than adults (on average, 9.25 hours). The trouble is that the body clock in your brain switches on a chemical called melatonin (to make you feel sleepy) at the same time of night as adults, but doesn't switch it off till later than adults in the morning. So, if you can't go to sleep till eleven or later at night, you will not get enough sleep on a school night and will still feel sleepy during the day. Sleep deprivation plays a huge part in stress and it's a vicious circle, because stress can stop you sleeping and not sleeping can be very stressful. It's like jetlag, every day of the week.

- **Depression.** We don't know why exactly, but teenagers experience about the same levels of depression as adults. You may find it harder to deal with because you have less life experience to teach you how to get help or to allow you to believe that life will get better.

Are All Teenagers the Same?

No! And I hate it when adults talk about young people as though they all have exactly the same emotions, worries or experiences. You are all going through adolescence, moving from being a child to being an independent adult, but you're also all different, individual. The differences come from: genes, gender, circumstances and life events, environment, personality, luck – many things you can't control.

One thing I believe unites very many teenagers is the feeling of not being in control. In many ways, you're not: you still usually have adults making rules for you. Part of the stress of being a teenager can involve feeling restricted, feeling that everything is unfair, that adults don't respect you, that you are trying really hard to do your best but your best doesn't seem to work. Lack of control is hard to deal with at any age. I believe that the attempt to gain control over your life is an important part of becoming an independent adult and one of the reasons why it is sometimes so difficult.

But there are things you can control. This book aims to give you some control back and to show you that you may have more than you think. Regaining some control over our lives is the best way to manage stress and prevent its negative effects.

Help! I don't find it stressful being a teenager! Am I weird?

No, just lucky! This book might show you some of the things your friends are worried about, though. It's also worth pointing out that different stages of adolescence can be harder or easier for different people.

What do parents (and carers) think?

Just as not all teenagers are the same, not all parents or carers are the same. Some cope better than others with the stresses of parenting. Some are better people than others; some are better controlled; some are cleverer; some are kinder. But the ones I come across really care and while I was writing this book I was overwhelmed by messages from them as they tried to help their teenage sons and daughters.

We parents know we're not perfect and we worry very much about getting it wrong. We won't always get it right, even if we try hard. And it's hard trying hard all the time.

Also, you have your biological changes turning you into a teenager, but parents move reluctantly from being the parent of a child (and in control of them) to being a parent of a teenager (and not being so much in control). It's not easy, believe me!

"My main feeling is one of helplessness and heartbreak that I can't put a sticky plaster on it and make my gorgeous girl all better, as I did when she was little."

Julia, parent

———————————

When you were little, your parents could make pretty much anything better. Now, when they see you hurting, they so want to help and sometimes they can't. Often, the reason they can't is that you won't let them. Sometimes you won't let them because you are embarrassed or because you think they don't care or because you think they can't help. Please try to let them help. And if your parents can't help or you really can't ask them, look for another adult who can. There are adults out there who want to help, I promise.

We often feel helpless. But even if we can't put a sticky plaster on it, there are things we can do. If you can, give us a chance.

SECTION TWO

Your Worries and Questions

Based on talking and listening to many teenagers, parents and teachers over the years, I've gathered common worries and questions, grouped them into topics and given suggestions and things to think about. The main aim of this section is to show you that you're not alone and to help you think about your situation in a constructive way, to see things in perspective.

When I was writing this book and talking to teenagers and their worried adults, I began to think that the worst thing about being a teenager is that when you have a worry you think no one else has the same worry. You think you're weird, or mad, or ill, or bad. You're not: your dark thoughts and habits are not unique. People out there share them. I want you to know that.

Strong and changing emotions are really common during adolescence. Your mood swings can be dramatic and feel out of control. You (and the adults around you) may feel very confused. It can make you feel bad about

33

yourself and you might worry that this is how you'll always be. Or perhaps you aren't even trying to look ahead but are just overwhelmed by what's going on now. But how do you tell what's normal and what may be normal but still require help? And how can you help yourself? I'm going to look at some common feelings and try to answer these questions.

"I think the biggest 'feeling' I recall from my teenage years is of being alone, feeling I didn't fit in. I was taller than everyone else for most of it. I never felt as trendy as anyone else or even pretty. I rarely opened up to my classmates. I spoke to no one, not even my family, about how I felt. Instead I buried my head in books and my writing. Having spoken to old school friends more recently, I now know that many of them felt that way. We had no idea that we were alone together."

Fiona, adult

"Why do I need to think about exams, getting a job and what I want to do with my future at this young age?"

Calum, 16

"I get stressed being asked what I want to do in

school and after school when I don't really know.
I just want to wait and see what happens."
Kyle, 16

————

"What stresses me most? Not living up to my
standards in exams and planning the future.
Social life is also stressful."
Christie, 16

————

"Being 16 and having to live the rest of my life
without parents is very stressful and makes me
feel very anxious."
Allison, 16

————

"Being youngest in my year and having
to get ready for uni."
Lauryn, 16

————

Before I go over some specific feelings, here's some general advice for dealing with any extreme emotions:
- ● Realize that adolescence affects your hormones, brain, biology and feelings. Remind yourself that this is not your fault.
- ● Learn about relaxation and caring for yourself. Try the suggestions in *SECTION THREE*.

- Talk to someone. There are adults who want to help and who know what you are going through.
- Remember that everything is a phase. You can get through this.
- Laugh! Laughter is one of the best ways to relieve stress and remove negative emotions.

Adolescence is often a time of extreme emotions, feelings which later seem quite irrational. But emotions are *supposed* to be irrational. Reason and emotion are opposite things and sometimes emotion overpowers reason. But if we didn't have emotions we'd be robots. The key to managing the difficult and emotional times of life is to recognise when we need to take time out, calm down and put our feelings into perspective.

For any of the problems that follow, also try some of the relaxation exercises and stress-management tips from *SECTION THREE*.

Feelings

Feeling angry

"I feel so angry a lot of the time."

"I snap at people and sometimes I throw things or lash out."

"Sometimes I feel the whole world is against me."

"I try really hard to do something right and it goes wrong so I get mad."

"I never used to feel like this – what's happening to me?"

Pretty much everyone feels angry sometimes. It doesn't mean you're a bad person. Some feelings of anger come from not being in control. Sometimes it really does feel as if the world is against you, when you try to do your best and things still go wrong or you get into trouble for something that feels unfair.

Anger is an instinctive reaction, a very powerful automatic response which begins in the emotional parts of your brain, particularly a part called the amygdala. The amygdala responds instantly and you feel a surge of anger before the more "thinking" parts of your brain have stepped in to rationalise or control it. We know that the amygdala and other emotional areas are well-developed in teenagers (in fact, from birth) but that the controlling prefrontal cortex is less well-developed.

Emotions are also affected by hormones, some of which go up and down wildly during adolescence in both boys and girls. An increase of testosterone, the mostly male hormone, can cause aggression and the desire to lash out and fight. And swings in levels of oestrogen and progesterone can affect emotions and behaviour in girls, sometimes leading to the very distressing condition called PMS. Hormones are powerful and important chemicals that we can't control by will-power, though we can learn to control our reactions. Once you realize that some of your feelings are caused by chemicals in your body and brain, you'll find it easier to predict when you'll feel bad and then you will be better able to control your reactions. Also, just knowing that something has a physical cause can make you less stressed about it.

So, anger is normal. But feeling angry very often or all the time is not a good thing; it will distract you from focusing properly and may harm relationships with friends and family. Not being able to control your anger and perhaps harming someone else or yourself is definitely something you want to avoid.

Continued anger is sometimes a sign of depression. Also, research suggests that boys and men often express depression through anger, perhaps more so than girls and women, whose depression looks more obviously like sadness and feeling low.

SUGGESTED STRATEGIES
AND THINGS TO THINK ABOUT:

- You can control yourself much better than you think. What I'm about to say may sound ridiculously simple and even a cliché but here goes: take three deep breaths and walk away from the situation. Reward yourself for doing this; each time you manage it your brain will learn more control and it will be easier next time. (When we try to do something, our brain actually builds the pathways between brain cells that eventually allow us to succeed.)

- When you feel angry, go somewhere where you can let it out safely without upsetting anyone else. Go for a run or a fast walk. Anger produces energy and you need to get rid of it. And yes, punching a pillow when you're angry does help – but not punching a wall!

- Talk to someone about what makes you angry. Talking to a neutral person can help put it into context.

- If you feel angry all the time or very often, see a doctor or talk to a trusted adult. It's not right that you should have to suffer so much. For girls,

39

feeling angry before each period is a symptom
of PMS, and doctors can help.

○ Try the relaxation exercises in *SECTION THREE*.

*"When you're feeling angry, channel that anger
into something creative. Write, paint, compose
music, whatever – but do something constructive
rather than destructive with it."*
Malorie Blackman, author

Feeling sad – is it depression?

"Sometimes I just cry and I don't even know why."

"It feels as if a thick black cloud is
pressing me down."

"I think I might be depressed – how do I tell
if I am?"

"I'm worried about a friend who seems
sad all the time."

There's a difference between feeling sad and having
depression. Feeling sad is a normal part of life. Sometimes

we know why we are feeling sad and sometimes we don't; both are normal. I'll come to dealing with grief and bereavement in a later section, because it's a special situation. What I want to talk about now is sadness and depression. Depression or "clinical depression" is a group of real illnesses which are quite different from just feeling sad because of something that's happened.

So, there are two real questions here: first, how can you tell if you or someone you know are suffering from depression (and, if so, what can you do about it) and second, if you're not actually suffering from clinical depression, how can you get over periods of feeling sad?

SOME SIGNS OF DEPRESSION

To be certain, you must see a GP because only they can assess you properly. Don't be scared or embarrassed to do this. GPs want to help. Here are the most usual symptoms but you may not have all of them and you may have some others:

- Feeling very sad most of the time for several weeks.
- Really low self-esteem: thinking you are useless, believing you are horrible or pointless.
- Not wanting to do anything; not enjoying things you normally enjoy.
- Not wanting to get out of bed. I don't mean just normal teenage sleepiness in the mornings. I mean

41

wanting to stay in bed and never get up.

- Lack of energy. On its own this isn't depression, but combined with some of the other symptoms it could be.
- Feeling hopeless about the future.
- Poor sleep: either trouble getting to sleep or waking early in the morning and then lying there worrying.
- Thinking about suicide or harming yourself.
- Weight changes and appetite changes. Usually, depression causes low appetite and therefore weight loss, but not always; sometimes people over-eat when they are depressed, and this is often called "comfort-eating".

You may also have heard of manic depression or bipolar illness. This is a type of mental illness which leads to dramatic swings between mania (thinking you are capable of anything and therefore sometimes taking huge risks) and depression (feeling hopeless, useless and sad). There are several different types of bipolar illness and other depressive conditions.

Depression can be mild, a background feeling allowing you still to cope with normal life; moderate, affecting your life quite badly; or severe, making it impossible for you to function.

It's important to realize that one of the problems with depression is that it can stop you being rational about yourself or your future; you may think nothing can ever help you get better. This means that you're not always the best person to make decisions about what to do; you'll need to trust your friends and family if they are trying to help you. I have tackled self-harming separately, so if you have concerns about yourself or a friend self-harming, please see that section.

If you think you might be suffering from depression:

- See a doctor. The doctor will assess you and recommend the right help. You might want to take a parent or other adult with you or you might prefer to go alone – it's entirely your choice.
- Make sure that the adults around you – at home and school – know what you're going through. Don't assume that they understand what you're feeling if you don't tell them.
- Recognise two very important things: this is not your fault; and there IS help.
- Your doctor will be in charge of your medical treatment but, as soon as you feel able to, there are things you can do to help yourself. Try any of the self-help advice in *SECTION THREE*. Being able to take some control over your life, by improving your nutrition and your exercise, for example, will be really helpful.
- Do any or all of the things in the next list, as well.

● If you ever have thoughts of taking your own life (or if a friend talks about this to you), get help immediately. Every young person's suicide is a tragedy and is never the right answer. Phone the Samaritans or Childline: the numbers are at the end of this book. They help, they really do. That's what they are there for.

SUGGESTED STRATEGIES
TO DEAL WITH FEELING LOW OR SAD:

● Exercise is one of the best ways to combat depression and sadness. Going for a walk in the fresh air is perfect exercise.

● Look after your nutrition. A good diet, with plenty of fresh food, boosts your immune system and gives you a sense of control, as well as making sure you have all the chemicals you need for good skin, bones, eyesight and brainpower.

● Find something to laugh about. Laughter has hugely positive benefits, releasing chemicals called endorphins around your brain, as well as taking your mind off whatever it is you are sad about. Keep your favourite funny DVD handy or watch a silly YouTube video.

● Stick with friends who make you feel good about yourself and avoid those who don't. We all know people who can make us feel bad about ourselves or who focus only on their own successes; avoid these people.

- Talk to a good friend about how you feel.
- For girls, if your feelings of sadness seem to coincide with the days before your period, a doctor will be able to treat you for PMS.
- Give yourself small treats or rewards. Having something to look forward to is a really good motivator. (There is more about this in *SECTION THREE*.)
- Eat dark chocolate! There's some evidence that dark chocolate has mood-lifting properties.
- Don't forget: how you feel now is not how you'll feel next week or next month or next year.

If you are worried about a friend, show her or him this advice. If your friend isn't able or ready to listen, talk to a trusted adult about your worries. Please remember that you are not responsible for your friend's health. I know this is a hard thing to accept, but you must not feel guilty, stressed or responsible if you are unable to help. You must look after yourself and your own life and health first.

"Schooldays AREN'T the happiest days of your life."
Sally Prue, author

"I was brought up with religion and was very strict on myself. My main memories are of feeling painfully self-righteous – it kept me thick-skinned and arrogant despite underneath feeling terribly insecure and fragile. [...] Feeling I had something to believe at least made me keep up the pretence of being 'together' when I was in fact choking what was deep inside. It gets better, but it's a long road!"
Hajar, adult

"I'm scared that I don't live 'that life', the one everyone wants to live. I don't know why I am so aware of it – I mean, I'm only 16. But that is what bothers me the most." **Ami, 16**

"I wish I had given out more compliments, so that maybe by focusing on someone else's good points, they might have reminded me of mine."
Catherine MacPhail, author

Feeling scared

Only a fool is scared of nothing. Being scared is what stops us doing stupid things, taking dangerous risks, putting our hands in fire, driving too fast, putting ourselves or others in danger for no good reason. But perhaps the most frightening things are the things we can't control, the things that might happen – but probably won't – the things we think we wouldn't be able to deal with, the things we feel would wreck our lives. Fearing them is normal but thinking about them too much can lead to negative and unhelpful stress. It can stop us functioning and enjoying our lives.

Young children are mostly protected from these fears. Adults can tell them not to be scared. Parents can say, "Don't worry, we'll look after you." And generally the young child then stops thinking about it.

As for adults, most of us have learnt three things: first, that the bad things we worry about usually don't happen. Second, that we can usually cope better than we imagine if they do. And third, that worrying about things that might not happen is a waste of energy and we'd be better spending our time focusing on things we can control. We still worry about them sometimes but can usually put them into a mental box called Things Not to Think About Too Much.

Teenagers are faced with these fears for the first time and this can make them seem worse. My big one when I was a teenager was war. I had vivid recurring dreams about it. I remember telling my parents and they said something like, "Don't worry, it probably won't happen." But that didn't stop me worrying, as it might have done if I'd been younger. My imagination made the fears worse

47

and I couldn't push them away as I can now I'm older.
Here are some fears you might have:

"I keep worrying about war/terrorism/death/illness."

"I'm worried about my
parents/siblings/friends dying."

"Someone I know died recently and it's
made me really scared."

"Everyone else seems to be so relaxed
about everything but I can't stop
thinking about bad things."

"I watched a film that really scared me
and I can't stop thinking about it now because
it could come true."

"I'm worried that I'll one day do something
really bad by mistake – and maybe cause
someone's death."

"I'm having constant intrusive thoughts about
horrible things happening."

These are perfectly reasonable things to be afraid of. They threaten to make your life sad or difficult. You worry whether you'd cope. Nearly everyone would worry. The problem comes if you let those thoughts take over. If you

48

do, you will waste time and energy thinking about things you can't control, time and energy that you could use to make good things happen in your life and actually enjoy yourself.

So, the key is to control what goes on in your head. How can you do this?

SUGGESTED STRATEGIES
AND THINGS TO THINK ABOUT:

- Accept that fear is a common part of growing up, that the things you are scared of will change and that what worries you now will fade.

- When one of the fears starts to take over, say "no" to it. In your head, say, "No, that's not worth thinking about." Visualise some method of brushing it away: a bulldozer removing the thought, fire burning it up, a brush sweeping it away. Keep this image and use it every time the fear tries to come back.

- Focus on other things to take your mind off bad thoughts. When the fear starts to intrude, force yourself to do something else: watch a favourite programme, play a computer game, read a book or magazine, phone a friend. Anything to occupy your thoughts. But going for a walk on your own *wouldn't* be the best idea because you might carry on thinking about the scary things.

● If you find you simply can't control these thoughts and they are interfering with your life, talk to an adult you trust. In extreme cases you might benefit from seeing a doctor who can put you in touch with a psychologist who can help you retrain your thinking.

● From the list in *SECTION THREE*, try relaxation techniques such as mindfulness, other forms of meditation or the suggestions for dealing with intrusive or negative thoughts. You might also investigate cognitive behavioural therapy (CBT), if your fears are really taking over your life.

● Avoid films or books that focus on the thing you are frightened of. In my advice about panic attacks I recommend facing your fears, but the fears I'm talking about here are different – they are most likely fears you won't have to deal with. Teenage novels often deal with these fears and many teenagers benefit from reading about them, but if you have a really bad fear I don't personally recommend tormenting yourself.

"When we think about the future most of us can only imagine the very immediate future, compared with when we were younger and making up ideas of what job we wanted,

and in some cases when we want to get married,
have children etc. Many of us will block out
thoughts of the future as we will never know
what the future holds for us."

Daryl, 17

"A lot of my friends and I are quite worried about
the future. I think we all feel these big decisions
have crept up on us, and we haven't got our heads
round them yet. Having said that, most of us are
looking forward to leaving school, to moving out and
creating a life of our own. It's just the uncertainty of
the future that worries us." **Isla, 17**

"I do [worry] with the current amount of people that
are unemployed and the lack of jobs available.
I'm also worried that there won't be anything left for
my generation, because of global warming."

Kirsty, 13

"The biggest worry is about the future: what's going
to happen when you leave school?"

Kirsty, 16

"I get stressed when I think about my future and
exams. I don't know what the future will bring."

Julie, 16

Feeling anxious

"I often feel really anxious – not about anything in particular, but I'm often just worried, like being nervous but there's nothing to be nervous about."

It's normal and positive to feel anxious when you're nervous about something particular. But sometimes you can get into a phase of feeling anxious a lot of the time and you may not even know what you're anxious about. This happens when your body doesn't switch off the stress chemicals but keeps them on a constant low level.

You may feel breathless, sweaty, a bit dizzy sometimes. You may lose your appetite or find yourself eating sugary foods more often. These symptoms can make it hard to concentrate at school or enjoy being with friends. And, because you're tense, you may get headaches or other pains.

"I'm stressed that I need to learn 4 to 5 dance routines, and one of them backwards, in just a couple of weeks, as well as trying to fit in time for studying and friends."
Jack, 16

———

"Lots of teenagers my age overthink things which leads to stress. They will come across a tricky

situation and then think about it too much, causing
them to not be able to stop thinking about it
and then all the worry leads to stress."

Kirsty, 13

SUGGESTED STRATEGIES
AND THINGS TO THINK ABOUT:

- Avoid any foods and drinks that can make symptoms worse: caffeine (in coffee and tea) and too much sugar, for example. Some people find that the artificial colourings and additives in fizzy drinks and sweets make them jittery or hyper. Try eliminating them and see what happens.
- Any exercise is an excellent way to lower anxiety and nervousness. Anything from a brisk walk to a martial art – anything that raises your heart rate and makes you a bit out of breath.
- Try yoga or other stretching exercises, combined with deep breathing.
- Looking at beautiful scenery can have a calming effect.
- See if you can work out what is making you anxious (though it may not be anything particular); talk about it with someone.

"Worry is a normal part of life, but if it becomes your life then something needs to change – exercise, see your friends, read a book, have fun – and if you can't cope, ask for help." **Kathryn, adult**

EXTREME ANXIETY – PANIC ATTACKS

"I have panic attacks – I actually feel I'm going to die."

"I'm scared of going to crowded spaces in case I have a panic attack."

"It happened at school and I felt really stupid – it's only happened once but I'm terrified it will happen again."

A panic attack is an extreme form of anxiety, which usually happens suddenly and with little or no warning. You may feel sweaty, breathless, sick or terrified – or all those things. It is an overwhelming feeling and you may even think you are dying. You aren't. You will probably worry that it might happen in a public place but if it did, most people would be very sympathetic. Anyone who teases a person having a panic attack isn't worth thinking about.

It's important to tell yourself that although panic attacks

are unpleasant, they're temporary and won't kill you. Your body and brain are over-reacting to a situation and telling you that they want your help; they need to rest and be cared for.

SUGGESTED STRATEGIES
AND THINGS TO THINK ABOUT:

- If you've never had a panic attack, don't worry about having one. Most people never have one. If you've had one before, remind yourself that no harm came to you and that you'll be able to deal with it better if it happens again.
- Learn good relaxation techniques and practise an anti-panic strategy, so that as soon as the first sign appears you can stop the panic happening. (See **Breathe Properly** in *SECTION THREE.*)
- It's important not to avoid the type of situations that might bring on an attack, otherwise your anxiety may turn into a phobia and you will find yourself restricting your life. But facing our fears is hard, so take this slowly. For example, have a friend with you and start with something not too worrying.
- Believe in yourself and realize that, even though it seems hard, you have the power to control these things. Everything you need is in your head.
- Read about anxiety disorders and panic attacks

online; you will find lots of good and reassuring advice and tips from people who have been through similar experiences.

⊙ If you're worried and need further help, see your GP.

Feelings of failure

"I'm not good at anything – I'm stupid."

"Suddenly I can't do things I used to be good at."

"We are supposed to say what we want to do when we leave school but I don't have anything I'm good at – the thought makes me panic sometimes."

"In primary school it was so easy and teachers always praised me – now I can't do anything right."

"Teachers think I'm not trying but a lot of the time I'm trying really hard."

"I've stopped trying because it doesn't make any difference – however hard I try, I can't do it."

"Everyone else seems to understand things better than me."

"I want to give up the subjects I can't do – I can't be bothered to try."

Part of the reason for these feelings is that, as a teenager, you're now more aware of what other people are doing. You know so much more about the world outside your own head; you see other people succeeding, you measure yourself against them, you start to worry about the future, and adults are no longer quite so protective. Adults may forget that you need encouragement, too. We all need it.

Also, if you're not yet at the stage of dropping your weaker subjects and focusing on your best ones for the last two years of school, you still have to struggle with things you're not interested in. Teachers have the job of pushing pupils to succeed in all subjects but many adults have forgotten what it's like to try hard and not succeed.

Personally, I think all adults should be forced to have the experience of learning something they aren't good at. A few years ago, I had oboe lessons for two years and it was a powerful reminder of what it's like to be a struggling learner, not an expert.

"As a teenager I didn't believe I was as attractive, smart or funny as my peers. Looking back I now realize I was all those things and wasted years doubting myself. Don't allow the low self-esteem trap to steal your confidence in yourself."
Joanne, adult

"I get stressed living up to the expectations of others. Why do I have to do so well?" **Asia, 16**

So, schools push you to do your best at everything, and when your best isn't good enough, it feels like failure. Most people experience failure at some point. Very few people are good at everything, though some lucky students are good at all the things that schools teach and measure.

But we shouldn't run from failure, even though it's tempting. It can be positive in several ways:

1. If we persevere and succeed, the feeling of pride is huge.

2. Practising hard makes things more firmly fixed in our brains so we are likely to keep a skill once we've got it.

3. Finding things difficult gives us a better understanding of other people and stops us thinking that we are the greatest people in the world. Modesty is not a bad thing. It keeps us human.

However, feeling that you are a failure can have negative consequences. It can stop you trying, blind you to your strengths and prevent you from achieving your potential and enjoying life, so I have some tips.

**SUGGESTED STRATEGIES
AND THINGS TO THINK ABOUT:**

● Because of the physical changes in the teenage

58

brain, you may experience a sudden loss of a skill that you previously had. This can be very upsetting and frustrating. But remember: the way the brain works is by practising. Continue to practise a skill and you can rewire the connections in your brain and get it back. So, be brave and keep trying – I promise it will help.

- Understand that there are many types of intelligence and only a few are tested in schools. So, you may find Maths, English or Science difficult but have other skills, and you should value them, even if you feel your school doesn't measure them and praise you. Look ahead to a time when your talents and your worth will be recognised. You may be "bad" at Maths (join the club!) but fantastic at creative ideas, planning events, inspiring younger children, leading a team or supporting others – all extremely important skills which will be useful in life after school.

- Remember that school success does not always equal life success. Many, many people who struggled at school go on to have extremely successful and happy lives. Many leaders in business, the arts and government did badly at school. Besides, not everyone wants to be a "high-flier" – having a job that pays the bills, friends and maybe a family is a fine way to live.

- Feeling stupid is a sign of intelligence! We're stupid if we think we know everything. Clever people understand that they don't know everything and do their best to focus on what they need and want to know.

- Try not to think about what other people can or can't do. You are almost certainly focusing on a few things that are going to make you feel bad about yourself.

- It's very encouraging to picture your brain cells growing new connections every time you try (even if you fail). This gives you a feeling of control.

- If you're struggling, ask for help. Teachers like to be asked – as long as you don't catch them when they are about to have a well-earned coffee. Choose a good moment or tell them that you are having problems and ask if you can arrange a meeting later.

- Ask a friend. If your friends don't understand either, you should all ask the teacher!

- Spend time doing something different or something you are good at each day. Swim or skate; play a computer game; play an instrument; play football with friends; volunteer in a charity shop; join a drama group; think about getting a part-time job. All these things and many more can give you a sense of worth and help you forget about things you find difficult.

● You are probably setting yourself ridiculously high standards. It's good to aim high but it needs to be something manageable. Set a lower goal and then, when you achieve it, aim higher again.

Feeling embarrassed

"I feel really self-conscious and hate it when people look at me."

"A really embarrassing thing happened recently and I wanted to die – I can't stop thinking about it."

"I didn't want to go into school after what happened so I've been bunking off."

"I dread being asked to speak in public."

"I hate having to write anything on the board at school."

Teenagers often experience embarrassment extra strongly. It feels as though everyone is looking at you and laughing. I still remember my huge embarrassment about things that wouldn't bother me at all if they happened now.

Compared with when you were younger, you are much more aware of people's opinions of you. A girl told me recently that when she became twelve she suddenly didn't know who she was any more. It's common to feel different from before, sometimes quite suddenly, and it can be confusing and make you think too much about what you look like and how other people see you.

You are also starting to experiment with new looks and images, and your changing body makes you extra self-conscious, too – I'll talk about that later, in **Bodies**.

Self-consciousness is normal. The good news is that it's most likely to get better as you grow older and more confident. The bad news is that while you're going through it, no matter how much I tell you not to be embarrassed, you will be!

"I somehow acquired a very bad stutter when I was 11 and felt very stressed and alienated. I got through by making people laugh with my drawings and had a pretend tattoo parlour (biro) at the back of the class, where all us 'naughty' girls were."
Nicola Smee, illustrator

You might be interested to know that embarrassment isn't all negative: your brain is now more developed so you can look at the world beyond yourself. Worrying too much is not helpful, but worrying a bit or at least considering what other people might be thinking will help you fit in. Or it will help you be different, if that's what you prefer, because not everyone wants to follow the crowd. Being conscious of your behaviour and how people see you is a step towards finding your place, your "look", your personality.

Scientists also know that teenagers process or think about embarrassment differently from adults, even using slightly different brain areas when facing embarrassing social situations. Perhaps this helps explain why adults are often not embarrassed about the same things as you, and why you may feel embarrassment more strongly.

SUGGESTED STRATEGIES
AND THINGS TO THINK ABOUT:

- Understand that this is all about perception – your perception. Everyone is *not* looking at you. The situation is far more important to you than anyone else.
- What you are horribly embarrassed about now will fade and feel better soon. Look ahead to that time.
- Practise the "putting the negative thoughts in a box" idea that I mention in **Feeling Scared**.
- If you're missing school or planning to, ask your-self, "Am I really going to let my embarrassment

63

affect my future?" If you go into school now, the embarrassment will fade when you face it. If you don't, it will be harder to go in later. Be brave and proud. If you can laugh it off or put a brave face on it, people will be impressed. And then they will forget about it.

● Ask yourself whether the thing you're embarrassed about is really that important. Don't people have to deal with worse things? Did anyone die?

BLUSHING

"I blush a lot – I mean a LOT!"

"I don't want to be in the school play because I know I'll start blushing."

Blushing is a way that your body lets excess heat out, usually when you're embarrassed and your heart rate has risen. Sometimes, the worst thing about blushing is worrying about blushing, which makes it more likely that you'll blush! For most people, it is a minor but annoying thing that happens when we're under pressure or on stage or when people are looking at us for some other reason. But for some people (teenagers *and* adults) it starts to take over their lives.

SUGGESTED STRATEGIES
AND THINGS TO THINK ABOUT:

- Try the relaxation or anti-panic techniques in *SECTION THREE*. Practise these before you need them, so that you can switch on the technique instantly.

- Remind yourself that everyone blushes some-times.

- Try online support groups for people who blush a lot or sweat too much (see **Sweating**, below). Sometimes, talking to or hearing about other people with the same problem can be enough to stop you feeling so bad.

- See your doctor if it's a real problem. They might refer you for a treatment to deal with the underlying thought processes causing the blushing or fear of blushing.

- There is special make-up for blushing, designed for men and women. It has a green tone, which will not make you look like the Incredible Hulk but disguises redness.

- In situations where you know you are likely to blush – for example, if you have to perform in front of the class – try not to focus on the blushing but on everything else about your performance; focus on the things you can control, such as making sure your notes are clear, and that you are wearing comfortable clothes. Do all that and you might forget to blush!

SWEATING

"I am always sweating – and that makes me embarrassed."

"I seem to sweat more than most people."

"My sweating is stopping me wanting to do things."

Sweating, like blushing, is a normal and necessary reaction to your body getting hot. Often, there are ways to control it, but occasionally people have a condition called hyperhidrosis, which literally means "too much water production". The excess sweating is most often on the palms, feet or armpits, but can also be on the back, groin, buttocks and face. This is very rare, affecting about 1% of the population, but if you think you might be one of those people, I recommend you see a doctor because there are treatments.

For "normal" excess sweating, here is some advice.

SUGGESTED STRATEGIES
AND THINGS TO THINK ABOUT:

● Wash regularly. I know, really obvious, and I know it doesn't really help on its own, but if you don't wash regularly then none of the other strategies will work either.

● Use a good anti-perspirant. It needs to be "anti-perspirant" and not just "deodorant" because a deodorant disguises a smell, rather than preventing the cause of it.

● Look out for an "extra strong" anti-perspirant – these are more expensive but many of them really do work. They come with special instructions; follow them carefully otherwise they can cause painful irritation. Some require you to put them on at night and wash them off in the morning. Some work so well that you don't even need to use them every day.

● Cotton clothing and underwear is better than synthetic because it allows heat to escape.

● When you know you're going to be sweating – for example, when performing on stage – choose your clothes carefully so that if you sweat no one notices. Clothes that are tight, or clothes that are mid to dark blue, brown or grey, make sweat more visible. Patterns – even subtle ones – are great at disguising sweat.

● If you are with your friends and you think you may have body odour, just say so. Then it immediately becomes less embarrassing.

● Everyone sweats! Don't let it ruin your life.

Specific Habits that Might Worry You

When people are stressed, they sometimes develop destructive habits. You may be embarrassed about a habit but still be unable to stop doing it.

Some habits are a symptom of OCD – obsessive-compulsive disorder. (I will talk about OCD separately, under **Special Physical and Mental Challenges**.) Others are simpler forms of stress. Others are just "odd things we do". We're allowed to do odd things!

Here are some habits people develop. They're not specially to do with being a teenager but the stress that you're under might make them happen at this time:

⊙ **Obsessive routines.** For example, washing your hands a certain number of times or in a certain way, or needing to touch something before you leave the house. These are typical signs of OCD but they don't necessarily mean you have that condition. Talk to a doctor about it.

⊙ **Pulling your hair out** – this is called trichotillomania. It can be the hair on your head, eyelashes or eyebrows, or all of them. (And trichotillophagia is the same but you actually eat your hair – not a good idea because it won't digest!) No one knows why trichotillomania happens but it is a type of compulsive (ie very hard to stop) behaviour often linked to stress. Since you don't really want to have bald patches, you'd probably like to stop. A doctor can refer you for therapy and there is help and reassurance online. See the resources section.

- **Skin-picking or any other destructive habit.** Most people do this a bit, and some naturally do it more than others. Nail-biting is particularly common and no one thinks this odd. But sometimes the picking goes beyond normal levels and when it gets to a certain point it is called excoriation disorder. There are the same sorts of treatment as for trichotillomania.

- **Sucking your thumb.** Most people stop this when they are younger, but some don't. Again, it's a compulsive behaviour and can be treated with one of the talking therapies mentioned in *SECTION THREE*.

- **Not washing** and caring for yourself. This can be a sign of depression so I recommend you see a doctor.

- If you're doing something I haven't mentioned, whatever it is, I guarantee someone else is doing it, too. If you're worried about it or want to stop, talk to a doctor or other trusted adult. There's help for everything.

HEARING VOICES

According to the international organisation for hearing voices, Intervoice, "around 8% of children and young people hear voices that other people don't." So, if you are one of them, you are not alone.

We all have conversations in our heads and sometimes "hearing voices" is just an exaggerated form of conversation in our head. For some people, it might be hard to tell the difference. It's also quite common, after something shocking such as when a loved one dies, to think you hear their voice. Although that's upsetting, it's nothing to worry about.

If the voices sound like someone speaking to you, from outside your head, it's a possible sign of illness. This illness can be temporary – perhaps just happening once and never coming back – or it can be more long-term. (Even schizophrenia can be a single episode.) But you do need to get it checked out because, as with most illnesses, it's far easier to treat if you catch it early.

So, if this happens to you, don't be frightened, but do investigate. A medical expert can show you how to deal with or eliminate your voices, and get to the point where they won't upset you.

Please don't suffer on your own.

SUGGESTED STRATEGIES
AND THINGS TO THINK ABOUT

- First, find out more about hearing voices and talk to other voice hearers, perhaps online. You'll find some resources at the end of this book. The Intervoice and Mental Health Foundation websites are reassuring. Intervoice has a section for young people, with a blog. It's a good place to learn about other people's experiences and to help you not feel alone.

- If the voices really do feel like voices speaking to you and telling you to do things, see a doctor. It's important to learn how to deal with these voices in a way that won't harm your health and to make sure that you have any necessary treatment early.

- Many people get used to hearing voices and come to see them simply as thoughts or conversations in the head, which, in a way, they are. But do consult a doctor first, rather than trying to cope on your own.

Bodies

Your changing body can cause a whole lot of stress. Even the bits that aren't changing can suddenly seem unattractive (to you) in a way that damages your whole self-esteem. For me, it was my knees... (Well, and the fact that I was too skinny, and skinny girls tend to be flat-chested. And then there was my nose. Of course.) My knee fixation wasn't helped by the fact that we had to wear skirts at school that were just above the knee. I used to try to force my knees to be straighter and I spent a lot of time looking at them in the mirror to see if they'd got more crooked than the day before. I'd even say to myself, in a kind of crazy way, "Never mind – one day I'll have a different life and in that life my legs will be straight." Actually, what happened was that one day I just stopped thinking that my legs were that bad. Also, I could wear trousers – hooray!

Anyway, I've separated some of the body worries into groups of similar concerns.

"When I was 14, I was so worried about wearing my swimsuit at the local pool in front of my friends and a boy I fancied that I didn't go once all summer. I missed out on loads of fun, laughs and excitement and felt really isolated. Your friends love you for

*who you are, not how you look in a swimsuit and if
a boy you like doesn't like your body then he's not
the boy for you."* **Cally, adult**

Developing bodies

"I am embarrassed about my body – I'm developing
earlier than my friends."

"I am embarrassed about my body – I'm developing
later than my friends."

Developing earlier – or later – than your friends can
be stressful. It can make you feel different, and people
may tease you because they don't know it bothers you.
A tiny comment can feel horrible. And most people, if
they knew you were hurt, would stop. (People who hurt
others deliberately are cruel or thoughtless. Avoid them.)

SUGGESTED STRATEGIES
AND THINGS TO THINK ABOUT:

● If you're developing earlier than your friends, try
to be proud of it, and remember that everyone
else will catch up and you'll forget there was
ever any difference.

73

- If you're developing later, I sympathise. That was me, too. As well as the genetic factors that you can't control, both diet and exercise make a difference, and they affect boys and girls differently. For boys, increasing testosterone is what makes you build muscle. Upper-body exercises and eating a good diet with enough protein will help – but you don't need protein supplements. For girls, being too skinny (through not eating properly) or doing too much energy-burning exercise can stop you developing breasts and can even prevent your periods starting or becoming regular. Extreme food and exercise behaviours can have long-term side-effects so do be careful. If you are doing serious sports training, whether boy or girl, make sure this includes good advice about a healthy diet.

- Stand tall and straight – whatever size you are, tall or short, well-built or not, standing straight makes you look and feel better and is good for your breathing and digestion.

Body hatred

"I actually hate my body, really hate it. I try to hide it."

"I spend a lot of money on make-up and clothes to make myself look good but it's not helping."

"I'm desperate to have surgery for my nose/breasts."

"I'm jealous of models in magazines."

I am sure your body is a lot more wonderful than you think it is! Most of us see our faults and ignore our strengths, particularly when we see photos of ourselves.

SUGGESTED STRATEGIES
AND THINGS TO THINK ABOUT:

- Before you compare yourself to models in magazines, please realize it's just clever computer software that blots out their blemishes, makes them thinner or curvier or smoother or whatever. They don't look like that in real life. And even the bits of them that are real look great either because they are phenomenally lucky or because they've spent hours and lots of money on them. Honestly, it's their job to look like that. They are part of a whole industry designed to make us buy stuff; there's no other reason for it.
- The bits of yourself you don't like can usually be disguised so that you don't notice them so much and you can emphasise your best bits instead.

75

It's in the mind. What you can't change, ignore. What you can change, well, if you can change it easily and cheaply (eg with make-up or different clothes) do, but if you can't, wait a few years and see if you still worry about it.

- As for surgery, put it out of your mind for now. See what you feel like when you're well into your twenties. By that time, the chances are that whatever it is you hate – small breasts, big breasts, crooked nose, skinny arms, whatever – won't be so obvious to you and you'll have learnt to see yourself more kindly and more proudly. If, on the other hand, you are still seriously upset about a part of your body that can be improved by surgery, see a doctor about it. But surgery is not really an option for most people: it's expensive, risky, painful and very, very often doesn't make you happy. (Very occasionally, it is the right answer, but you've a whole load to think about first and you'll need to wait until you are an adult, unless it's a medical situation.)

"At seventeen all I could see in the mirror was an ugly wide nose and awful moustache, spots and bags under my eyes, lop-sided breasts and knobbly knees.

I see photos of my teenage self now, and think,
I was gorgeous and I had no idea! "

Emma, adult

"*I wish I had thought more about my good points
and not my faults. I hated my hands. They were full
of blue veins and I had knobbly knuckles.
Now, I realize my hands run in the family. I had my
granny's hands. Something to be proud of not
ashamed of. Wish I had realized that then.*"

Catherine MacPhail, author

"*My memories of teenage stress (aged 15–16):
that my hair was never ever going to look right; that
the world was going to end because of an atomic
explosion; that I was fat; that there was no
one else in the world the same as me; that
everyone else seemed to have a plan and I didn't…
As you can see, a very neurotic child. What do I
know now (aged 47)? That actually people don't
really look at you with the same scrutiny that you
impose on yourself – no one notices
the bad hair days…* "

Lorna, adult

TEETH

"I hate my teeth – they are crooked."

"My teeth are yellow – I want gleaming white ones!"

"I'm 16 and I really need my teeth done – have I left it too late?"

If you hate your teeth it can affect how you interact with people, because you may avoid smiling or being in photos. Believe me, I sympathise. But many, many people think their teeth are worse than they are, and the chances are that no one else has noticed what you don't like about yours. However, the teenage years are a good time to fix them if you need and want to.

SUGGESTED STRATEGIES
AND THINGS TO THINK ABOUT:

- Crooked teeth can be sorted at any age and are often dealt with when you are a teenager. Many of your friends probably have braces. Ask your dentist about it next time you go for a check-up, which you should be doing once or twice a year. Or make an appointment earlier than that. The work will either be carried out by your dentist or by a specialist orthodontist.

- In the UK, treatment is free if you are under 18

and if you genuinely need the work to be done. Your dentist would need to agree, but in practice they are keen to support you improving your teeth. Usually, you need to be at least 12 or 13, but it does depend.

- Other problems, such as staining, can also be dealt with, though many dentists are against tooth-whitening treatments. Teeth are not naturally gleaming white, so anyone you see with very white teeth has had them artificially whitened. Tooth whitening is not simple and you should take expert advice and not do anything yourself, such as buying a product your dentist doesn't approve of. Trust a dentist more than a company trying to sell you something.

BAD BREATH

"I have bad breath - it seems to be much worse than everyone else's."

"I am not sure if I have bad breath but I worry that I have."

"I can't drink coffee at all because of the smell afterwards."

"I use breath sprays but they don't last."

Bad breath is called halitosis and everyone has it some-times. No one likes it – either having it or being near someone with it. Breath sprays don't work for very long, and are expensive. Eating a mint sweet will give only a very temporary relief – and will be bad for your teeth unless it's sugar-free.

If you are cleaning your teeth properly, after breakfast and at night, but you still have bad breath or a horrible taste in your mouth, here are some possible causes and suggestions.

SUGGESTED STRATEGIES
AND THINGS TO THINK ABOUT:

- Raw onions, garlic, curry and coffee can all affect your breath but we wouldn't want to do without them. If your breath smells of them, cleaning your teeth only helps temporarily, because the smell is mostly coming from your throat and oesophagus (food-pipe). Eating raw parsley is supposed to help. But the easiest thing is to keep drinking water and wait till your food has digested.

- When you're hungry, your body starts to burn fat and a by-product of that is a bad taste and smell in the mouth. I call it hunger-breath. Obviously, the solution is to eat. Mint chewing-gum and drinking water also help.

- Mouth or tooth infections cause bad breath. It would be a good idea to ask your dentist if it doesn't get better after a few days. You can try using a mouthwash, but if it's a real infection you may need something stronger, which you shouldn't use too often or you'll kill the "good" bacteria in your mouth as well.

- Gum disease – gingivitis – makes your gums swollen and tender or sore, and may make them bleed. It's the result of plaque building up and can cause bad breath partly because it makes it sore to brush your teeth properly. Your dentist can help you prevent it.

- Having a cold or other minor illness can also give you bad breath. Keep drinking water and wait till the cold is better.

- Are you really cleaning your teeth properly? You need to floss in between your teeth, too, or use an "interdental" brush. And you need to keep your tongue clean. There are some special tools for that, or you can get a toothbrush with a side designed for tongue-scraping. Euuw!

- As with my suggestion for worrying about sweating, I find that saying, "Sorry about the garlic breath, guys – I ate some really garlicky pasta last night" is helpful. You can't do it every day, though...

ACNE

"It's not all over my face but I know I'll have one or two huge spots most of the time."

"I have bad acne - really bad."

"I spend so much on cleansing things but nothing makes a difference."

Acne - spots on the face and often also on the back - is such a common problem and a real blight on many teenagers' lives. Just at the time when you want to look your best, and maybe attract a boyfriend or girlfriend, you find unattractive spots breaking out on your face. Nature is really not fair sometimes.

It's possible to get acne at any stage of life but it's much more common for teenagers, so do focus on the fact that yours will most likely disappear soon. It is almost certainly caused by hormones, not diet or poor hygiene. However, good hygiene is an important part of trying to control it.

You will probably find your acne goes in phases. It may be worse when you're stressed and girls may find it's worse just before a period. I did say Nature wasn't fair...

SUGGESTED STRATEGIES
AND THINGS TO THINK ABOUT:

● You'll know this already, but the first step is good

skincare, cleansing your face morning and night, using products designed for oily skin and acne. Don't rub your face too hard as this can make it produce more oil.

- Next, speak to a trained pharmacist at the chemist. (Go to the prescriptions counter and ask to speak to the pharmacist. You might be embarrassed if there are other people around so wait for a quiet moment or ask to speak privately – they should have somewhere you can go.)

- See your doctor. Doctors are very sympathetic to young people with acne and there are a number of good treatments they can prescribe. Some become less effective after a while, so go back to your doctor and try a new one. New products are coming out all the time.

- There is at least one acne pill which can cause low moods as a side-effect. These can have disastrous consequences, and young people have even committed suicide. It's really important to follow the instructions your doctor gives you. Tell your friends and family to look out for your mood becoming worse.

- If acne is making you genuinely depressed, tell your doctor.

- Try not to squeeze spots – you might leave a scar. I know it's tempting. Gently using two cotton buds is fine but if you have to apply much pressure, don't do it.

○ Make-up doesn't help and can make acne worse. Of course there will be times when you want to use it but try not to unless you absolutely have to. Look for make-up that is "non-comedogenic"; this means that it won't block pores.

○ Don't be tempted to take any medicine that has not been either prescribed by a doctor or is available from a pharmacist. (See next point.)

○ There are some alternative therapies you might want to try, such as Chinese medicine, herbalism, acupuncture or homeopathy. It's important to remember three things: first, not all of them are scientifically proven (though they may still work). Second, just because something is "natural" doesn't mean it is definitely safe, so do, please, still take advice from trusted adults before taking any treatment. Third, sometimes treatments interact badly, so always tell any therapist (and your doctor) what else you are taking.

○ Sunlight treatment (and sun-lamps) used to be prescribed for acne but it's not now recommended because of the risk of permanent damage or skin cancer. Don't be tempted to use tanning salons.

○ Foods containing chemicals called antioxidants

help keep your skin healthy. Look out for foods which naturally have bright colours, such as tomatoes and blueberries. Also foods that are rich in Omega-3 fatty acids, such as oily fish.

Weight problems

"I feel fat - people tell me I'm not, but it's about how I feel, isn't it?"

"I'm overweight but I just don't seem to be able to lose it. I never used to have a problem."

"I diet and exercise a lot and some people say I'm overdoing it. But how can you have too much exercise?"

"I guess I'm not technically fat, but I feel fat because I used to be skinny. I hate my new body."

OK, obviously I can't see you, so I don't know if you're overweight. But there's an easy way for you to find out: ask your doctor. If you are, your doctor won't lie because he or she will want to encourage and help you to achieve a healthy weight. If you're not, you should believe your doctor and not go on a diet.

Remember that your body is changing a lot and for girls this means becoming curved in places that might have been skinny before. Sometimes, our perception is faulty and we think we're fat when we're really not. (I will talk about the extreme version of this, body dysmorphia, in the section on **Eating Disorders**.) It can take a while to get used to your new adult body shape.

SUGGESTED STRATEGIES
AND THINGS TO THINK ABOUT:

- First, check with a doctor whether you are a healthy weight for your height and age.
- Remember that you are growing and that growth happens in bursts. If you've changed a lot in the last six months, that doesn't mean you will change the same amount in the next six.
- Accept that you can't stay a child forever and that soon you will grow to know and appreciate your new nearly-adult shape.
- Exercise and eating a good diet including lots of fruit, veg, wholegrains and protein, and not too much processed or fast food, is a good idea for everyone (see SECTION THREE). Over-exercising or using extreme dieting techniques are really bad ideas. They can cause physical and psychological damage.
- If you research dieting on the internet, be very careful what you believe. Many teenagers (and adults) enjoy the feeling of control that going

on a successful diet can give them; you need to be incredibly careful not to let it get out of hand. (See the section on **Eating Disorders**.)

SUMMING UP HOW TO DEAL WITH BODY PROBLEMS

- Realize that many people – especially teenagers – don't like their bodies. You are not alone.
- Realize that other people don't see what you see – you see all your "faults" much more than anyone else.
- Realize that you're changing fast and you'll soon grow into your new body and get used to it.
- Look after your diet and skin – but not in an extreme way.
- If you are really stressed about anything at all to do with your body, see a doctor or speak to an adult you trust.
- Don't let dissatisfaction with your body ruin your life. We're all given different advantages. Focus on your best bits.
- Anyway, looks are not everything. Think of all the other things that help us be who we are and help us succeed in life. Would you rather have a plain or unattractive body and a great personality, or a gorgeous body but be so mean no one wants

to know you? And which one of the two can you
actually do something about? Being nice can last
you all your life.

Eating Disorders

The most common eating disorders are anorexia nervosa
(when you don't eat enough, and may exercise too much)
and bulimia nervosa (when you "binge" on food and then
feel guilty and make yourself sick, or take laxatives to give
yourself diarrhoea).

Both are dangerous and need expert help. If you don't
get help, both these conditions result in long-term health
problems. In extreme circumstances, you can even die,
because our bodies need the right food to function.

Sometimes, a person's perception of their own size
is completely different from reality and everyone else's perception. In extreme cases this is called body dysmorphia.
If you think you are fat but everyone keeps telling you
you're not, check with a doctor, who will weigh and
measure you and tell you the truth, based on written
guidelines. If your perception is getting in the way of health
and happiness, your doctor will suggest some therapy,
which will probably involve CBT.

Boys get eating disorders, too, though they're more
common in girls, who are often more focused on their

appearance and more often the targets of the fashion industry. But note that anorexia isn't only about weight and food; it's also about control and unhappiness. Eating disorders are complicated things with many different forms and reasons.

Here are some signs that you may be suffering from an eating disorder:

- Do you think you're fat even though people say you're not?
- Do you feel frightened of putting on weight or being fat?
- Do you tell lies about what you've eaten or pretend that you've eaten when you haven't?
- When you have eaten, do you then immediately exercise to avoid putting on weight?
- Do you feel powerful and good when you go for a few hours without food or do too much exercise?
- Do you ever make yourself sick or take laxatives to try to lose weight?

If the answer to even a few of those questions is yes, it is really important that you talk to a doctor. You may be worried that they'll tell you to eat more but doctors do understand that it is far more complicated than that. A doctor is a very important start to getting help and support for you.

How do eating disorders affect teenagers especially?

Eating disorders commonly start during adolescence, though younger children are sometimes affected. One possible reason is that you are being bombarded with pictures of stick-thin models, just at a time when your body is changing and you are at your most vulnerable.

Also, as I say, eating disorders are not merely about food; they are also about mood and feelings. Depression is common amongst teenagers and if you're feeling sad, overwhelmed, out of control in some areas of your life, food can seem to be one area where you can be in control. The trouble is that you end up being out of control, though you still think you're in control.

As you change physically towards being a woman or man, it can be hard to like your body. You feel it is taking over, developing without your permission – which it is! Psychologically, you might try to fight your body by controlling what food it gets.

But, whatever the reason, it's vital to get treatment and help. It's a medical condition, and a serious one.

**SUGGESTED STRATEGIES
AND THINGS TO THINK ABOUT:**

● Please see a doctor – either your GP or a clinic aimed at young people. And if you don't feel that the first doctor you see is properly listening, see another one.

- Try to allow the adults in your life to help. It's upsetting for them, but they will find it much more upsetting if they can't help you.

- You probably enjoy the feeling of control over your body but in fact anorexia and bulimia are illnesses and *they* are trying to control *you*.

- Warning: please ignore websites, blogs and chat rooms that give the idea that anorexia is a good thing. It's not. It's dangerous. Being very underweight is unhealthy, just as being very overweight is.

- If you're worried about a friend who you think has an eating disorder, the first step is to show that you're worried. If your concern is rejected, the best thing I can suggest is to ask for advice from an adult you trust. You don't have to say who you are worried about.

Self-harming

"I sometimes hurt or cut myself – I like the feeling but I'm embarrassed, too."

"I can't explain why I do it – I want to stop but I can't."

"It makes me feel in control."

"Cutting myself stops me feeling sad about things."

"When I cut, I stop hurting everywhere else."

Self-harming can be cutting, burning or any form of deliberate harm. When parents discover that a son or daughter has been self-harming, it's really difficult for the parent and for the young person. Parents may react very strongly, through sadness or fear, and the huge wish that it hadn't happened. But they need to understand that it does happen and that you need their support.

Self-harming is risky; it can cause serious injury. But there are many reasons why people do it and sometimes, once you start, it's hard to stop. It is usually a reaction to sadness, stress, grief, or any kind of emotional pain. Some self-harmers feel that the pain of hurting themselves takes the emotional pain away for a while. This could be because pain releases chemicals called endorphins, described as "happy chemicals". Some enjoy the pain because they say it is better than a feeling of emptiness. Some feel it gives them control when they have very little other control in their lives. It is sometimes a cry for help but more often the self-harmer will keep it secret.

However, it's hard to keep scars secret forever and most self-harmers regret doing it, because when the pain has gone the scars are still there.

So, I'd like to help you stop. Whatever you've done

already, put it behind you and don't blame yourself. You can't change the past. Let's look at how to help you not do it again.

SUGGESTED STRATEGIES AND THINGS TO THINK ABOUT:

- Talk to someone about it. If you don't want to tell a parent, choose another adult, or a friend you trust. More people have heard of self-harming nowadays, and, even if your friend doesn't know what to say or do, perhaps together you can find a way to get help.

- Self-harming can be part of depression, so follow the advice given in that section.

- Talk to an expert. The organisation MindFull has trained online counsellors who focus on helping young people who are self-harming. Ask them (or your doctor) about dialectical behaviour therapy, which is recommended by the NHS for self-harming.

- Plan avoidance strategies to take your mind off the urge to self-harm. Then, each time you feel the urge, use one of them: for example, phone a friend, go for a walk, watch TV with your family, put some music on, do some yoga.

- Remove the items you use for self-harming, so that you can't see them or get at them easily.

Sometimes the urge to self-harm passes quickly and it just requires you to find a distraction for an hour or so, or maybe even less.

- Reward yourself for not doing it for a day, then two days, then a week, then a month. Self-harming can be addictive, so treating it like an addiction is a good strategy.

- Instead of harming, express your emotions in another way: draw, paint or write – maybe a letter to yourself, or an emotional poem. You can rip it all up afterwards; no one needs to see.

- Remind yourself that your feelings will change. The scars could be permanent so try to find something to do that won't cause permanent damage. Pinching yourself would be better than cutting, for example.

- Be optimistic: it's believed that around 90% of young people who get proper help stop self-harming within a year.

- Be very careful about blogs, groups or sites set up by people who are themselves self-harming. Some actively encourage you to self-harm more and even try to make it seem glamorous. Sometimes there are really nasty conversations which have occasionally led people to think about or commit suicide. Instead, focus on sites set up by experts or those who have beaten the problem.

The only good advice is advice that tries to help you stop hurting yourself and live a happier life.

● Take comfort from the thought that there is help for you. You just have to be brave enough to ask for it.

"She has low self-esteem, and is taking some risks. Yesterday I discovered she has been self-harming, which came as a huge shock, as she tried it once before then told me she would never do it again, so I hadn't been looking for it. I have been concerned for some time she may be bordering on depression, as she is often very low and her grades are suffering. She is gorgeous, but doesn't think she is, and worries about her weight/appearance. The peer group she is in is pretty foul and there is a lot of emphasis on appearance, and with boys massive pressure to experiment sexually. She does talk to me, but I am aware she isn't telling me everything."

Julia, parent

WORRIED ABOUT A FRIEND SELF-HARMING?

"A friend of mine harms herself and I don't know how to help her."

This is a tricky situation – especially if you discovered this by chance and your friend didn't actually tell you – but it's important to try to help. First, try to talk to your friend about it. They might be angry or try to deny it but if you continue to say that you are worried and you care, you should be able to break through the barrier. There is excellent advice on the website kidshealth.org, and some detailed strategies there. But one thing I'd add is that you must not take all the responsibility for your friend's health. You are young, too, and you have your own problems to deal with. Show your friend you care and make sure he or she realizes that there is help available, really good help.

If you're worried and don't know what to do, talk to a trusted adult, especially a teacher, who will be trained in how to respond.

There are great resources at the end of this book.

Relationships

Friends

The teenage years are when relationships with friends change and difficulties can crop up. There are many reasons. Moving to secondary school may break off some old friendships. Growing up means changing; you and your friends may change in different ways, starting to like or dislike different things from each other and from before. People mature differently. Also, when you were younger some of your friendships were created by your parents. For example, you may have "gone round to play" with the children of their friends, but not because you chose them.

"I get stressed about things changing with friends: losing friends and getting dragged into fallouts."
Fay, 16

"My biggest worry about the future is losing my friends once I have left school."
Andrew, 16

You are changing, too, with new views about what you want, how you feel and who you are comfortable with.

When you're a teenager, there's a lot of competition for status, competition about physical appearance, competition to be "cool". There's pressure either to be different or to fit in. Human beings are incredibly complex creatures and all the things that combine to create and maintain friendships are not things anyone can control. So, a lot of the friendship stuff is no one's fault at all.

"I wasted a lot of time worrying about what my friends would think rather than being myself."
Pete, adult

"I remember finding it very hard to make friends being the only new girl in a Spring term. People assume because you're not ugly, quite clever and good at sport that you must be happy and full of yourself but in fact you just want to make friends like everyone else and people don't want to be your friend." **Susan, adult**

"I knew I'd never fit in with the people who wore high heels and make-up. So I read Sartre and acquired a taste for black coffee and angst. I didn't realize Simone de Beauvoir did all four until it was too late. Don't choose, do it all!"
Anne Rooney, author

"As an early teenager I was one of those awful shrieking performing girls who has nothing to say yet, so covers it up with a lot of noise. As a late teenager I was quieter, because I was mired in an unhealthy relationship that ate away at what little self-esteem I had. All anyone had to do was look at me with kindliness and interest and I would dissolve in helpless tears."

Margo Lanagan, author

On top of friendship issues, there are new feelings of being physically attracted towards a boy or girl. These are powerful and distracting emotions which I'll talk about later.

All these changes are a necessary part of finding out who you are and who you want to be. You can't affect that process, but you can recognise some of the problems and find ways to make them better or make yourself feel better.

"Sometimes my best friend says hurtful things to me – she doesn't seem to like me any more."

Has this started recently? Do you think she's doing it on purpose or does she perhaps not realize she's hurting you?

99

There are several things to consider first.

Perhaps she's wrapped up in her own stresses and taking them out on you, without meaning to. Perhaps you haven't shown her you're upset? It's possible you're being over-sensitive: teenagers often misunderstand body language and expressions. Maybe she's jealous, even subconsciously; even good friends are sometimes jealous of each other. And sometimes people push each other to get a reaction, to test boundaries. It's also possible that you've accidentally done something to upset or annoy her.

SUGGESTED STRATEGIES
AND THINGS TO THINK ABOUT:

- Let your friend know she's upsetting you. If she is doing it on purpose, the friendship is fragile, I'm afraid, and that's not the behaviour of a real friend. But if she hasn't noticed, she needs to know. If you've done something to upset her by mistake, you need to know so that you can apologise or explain. It could be a complete misunderstanding!

- If a friend starts to be annoyed by you (or the other way round) then the friendship maybe needs a break. You may drift apart. This is a sad and sometimes stressful thing but entirely natural. The problem with schools is that everyone is so close together, seeing each other all the time, whether they like it or not. In the "real" world, friendships strengthen and weaken more naturally and gradually, with no one getting upset. In the wider world, people gravitate towards or away from each other without it being a big deal, but in schools it often *is* a big deal.

● The main thing to remember, when friendships change or end, is that it's about the chemistry between both of you. It's no one's "fault". Move on and find new friends.

● On the other hand, many good friendships survive rocky patches and arguments. Just be cool about it and be there for your friend if she comes to you.

"I had a terrible argument with a friend and we don't talk any more."

My strategies for this would be similar to the point above. However, what you first have to work out is whether this is a friendship you want to save. Then, you need to think whether you still feel angry and hurt and maybe whether your friend still feels angry or hurt.

If any or all of these things are the case, then you need to find a way to solve the problem. Pick your time – preferably when things have calmed down a bit – and arrange to talk to your friend in a neutral place. Obviously, how this pans out will depend on three things: what the argument was about and whether one of you did something to cause the problem; how willing or able your friend is to discuss and apologise or forgive; and how willing you are to discuss and apologise or forgive.

One thing to consider: saying sorry can often make the person who says it feel a whole lot better, as well as the person they say it to. Even if you feel that the argument was mostly your friend's fault, opening the discussion with an apology can make all the difference. For example, if you were really angry, you might have said something over the top, even if it seemed justified at the time. An apology – a genuine one – is a very brave thing to do but also extremely helpful.

If you apologise and your friend rejects the apology, then at least you tried. I believe genuine apologies should almost always be accepted. That doesn't mean everything is forgotten, just that the person accepts that the other one is sorry.

If, after trying to sort the situation out, your friend still won't talk or makes your life difficult, then in my opinion the best strategy for you is to remain calm, mature and patient. If this friendship is over, then it's over and you'll move on and make other friends. Life will go on and the situation will gradually feel less stressful.

"I don't feel my friends think like I do."

"I feel so different, so awkward. I never know what to say."

"I find it hard to make friends."

All these feelings are incredibly normal, and adults have them, too. (Younger children tend not to analyse it like this: they just "feel", without being able to put words to it as well as teenagers and adults.) It's especially true for sensitive people (and being sensitive is a good thing because it means you care) and for people who worry more than others. There are so many different types of people in the world and you are just finding out who you are and who you feel comfortable with. There are lots of possible reasons but you certainly shouldn't blame yourself. Whoever you are, and whatever you like, there are people out there who can be your friends. It just happens that unfortunately they aren't the people who are around you at school. But school is not forever.

SUGGESTED STRATEGIES
AND THINGS TO THINK ABOUT:

- It's likely that lots of other people in your class are thinking the same.
- You may be over-analysing or having impossible standards of perfection. Friendship is often about

compromising and no one is perfect.

- Maybe you just haven't found your true friends yet.
- You may be maturing faster (or more slowly) than your peer group and this is making you feel disconnected.
- Having different interests and likes is natural and good. You can always meet up with people with similar interests outside school, too.
- Be patient – this could be a very short phase.
- Some people are more private than others and find it difficult to relax in large groups. So, enjoy the times when you are with someone you like and spend more time with one or two friends rather than a large group.
- You may be suffering from self-consciousness – see the section on **Feeling Embarrassed**.

"A friend is having real problems right now and I don't know how to help."

"I know someone whose cousin committed suicide recently and I find myself worrying about my friends any time they feel sad."

Good friends worry about each other and you should feel proud that you care so much. Your friends will value this, even if they are too wrapped up in their problems to think about thanking you at the moment. But there's an important saying, that if you don't care for yourself you can't care for other people.

I was talking recently to pupils who had a friend who had taken her own life. Many of them had started worrying whenever anyone said they felt depressed. So one of the teachers gave a talk to the whole year, saying that they must not take on the responsibility of their friends' happiness and mental health. It was a very valuable message: yes, you must care, but you cannot take the whole responsibility.

SUGGESTED STRATEGIES
AND THINGS TO THINK ABOUT:

- Make sure your friend knows you are there to help. You don't have to keep saying, "Are you all right?" or, "What's wrong?" You can say, "You seem really down – if you want to talk, I'm here."

- Try to think of things to do together – going to the beach, seeing a film, going shopping, going for a run – but don't push if your friend doesn't want to.

- If you're worried, talk to an adult you trust. Just say, "I'm really worried about *** – what do you think I should do?"

- Most people who feel sad aren't suffering from

depression and most people with depression don't commit suicide.

● If you think your friend is trying to get attention, give them some! A cry for help is a cry for help and we need to answer it.

● Don't blame yourself if you do the wrong thing when you were trying to do the right thing. It's what you tried to do that matters and you can't foresee the future or be responsible for what other people do.

SECTION TWO

"I don't really like being with other people –
I prefer being alone – but is it weird or wrong
to be like that?"

Being comfortable on your own is a good thing. Some people are only happy in large groups and others prefer smaller groups or just talking to one person at a time. It might be a confidence thing and later, when you are with people you relate to better, you may change. Meanwhile, if you enjoy being on your own, that's fine. It's not weird or wrong. But don't cut yourself off entirely because friendship does need a bit of effort on both sides. However, being a good friend does not have to mean being life and soul of the party. We need quiet, thoughtful people, too.

"Sometimes I go along with what my friends
do even though I don't like it."

"Some of my friends are doing something
I think is a really bad idea – I want to tell them
but I'll lose their friendship."

It's so easy to go along with stuff because you want to be part of a group. I remember doing that often and I wish I hadn't. If you can, be strong, stand up for what you really believe. That's often very hard to do. I don't blame you if you don't manage it but I admire you if you do.

GENERAL ADVICE FOR DEALING WITH FRIENDSHIP PROBLEMS

- Understand that teenagers often misinterpret what others are thinking. This is explained by a physical brain difference and you get better at it once your prefrontal cortex develops.
- Remember that emotions are often harder to control when you're a teenager; when you say the wrong thing, just say sorry and don't beat yourself up about it.

- Look ahead to the future, when you've left school; you'll have a whole new world of people to find friends in.
- See also the sections on *Social Media and Phones* and *Bullying and Cyber-bullying*.

"True friends last a lifetime."
Malorie Blackman, author

Sexual attraction

Readers of this book are all different ages, at different stages of development. Some of you will still be cringing at the very thought of sex and others have raging hormones making you think about it a lot. Some of you will want it and others won't. In the UK, the age at which a young person is allowed by law to have sex is sixteen – *both* partners must be at least sixteen – but you need to be able to discuss the topic earlier than that, so that you are informed.

Fortunately for me, it's not my job to tell you anything much about the act of sex or how to do it. Anyway, you're probably already reading magazines that will answer a million detailed questions about love, sex and relationships, and they can do it better than I can in one short book. I think magazines focusing on your specific age group are a good way to get a whole range of views about what's right and wrong and what works and what doesn't.

Apart from the law, there are cultural and religious differences in what is acceptable when it comes to physical attraction and sex. The last thing I want to do is offend anybody but I also can't take every viewpoint into consideration. If you belong to a culture or religion which makes it very difficult for you to be open with your family about what you are going through, then you need to find good advice that suits your own position. Finding a trusted adult for you means finding one who understands your culture, while respecting the laws of this country.

Anyway, sexual attraction involves a lot more than actual sex. You can do a lot without actually having sex, and if you don't want it yet it certainly doesn't mean there's anything wrong with you. There really isn't! Not wanting sex until much later is perfectly natural and normal and healthy.

I want to cover a few fairly general points which can cause stress, to reassure you, to stop you feeling worried and alone, and to point you towards more detailed advice.

At the back of this book, you'll find suggested resources to explore these areas more.

"What stresses me most about being a teenager is everyone losing their virginity while you sit in a corner not knowing what half the stuff actually is."
Charlotte, 16

***

"I was always so nervous when I met a boy, especially one I liked. I was tongue-tied or else said the daftest things. I wish I had known that they were probably just as nervous as I was. Then I would have been able to concentrate on making them feel at ease."
Catherine MacPhail, author

***

SHYNESS OR FEELING INADEQUATE

"I can't stand the idea of taking my clothes off in front of a boy/girl."

"I don't know what to do – what if I make a fool of myself?"

Inhibitions about taking clothes off are entirely natural and healthy. Don't do anything you don't want to do; take advice from friends and age-appropriate magazines; be as confident about your body as possible; and realize that most people are shy like this.

Also, forget the images of the "perfect body" you see in the media. Hardly anyone in real life has a body like that and, as I said in the section on **Bodies**, models in magazines look like that largely because of clever lights, make-up and computer software.

It doesn't matter if you don't know what to do. If both partners don't know what to do, you can work it out together. If one does, he or she can teach the other one. As long as you only ever do what you are entirely comfortable with, you feel completely ready for it emotionally and you keep yourself safe, and as long as you are both past the age of legal consent (sixteen in the UK), that's what's important.

RESPECT – OR NOT

"Respect yourself. If you don't, why should anyone else?" **Malorie Blackman, author**

Decent human beings treat each other decently, with respect and empathy. Anyone who doesn't needs to be shown that their behaviour is unacceptable and will not be tolerated. And it doesn't matter what your religion or culture: the situations I'm about to mention are unacceptable.

I would also like to say that, partly because of the

111

huge increase in online porn and the fact that boys are very often viewing it before they are sexually active, too many boys and young men think sex must be violent and aggressive, with women treated as objects. This is not how it's supposed to be. It should be an act between two people who want and deserve to enjoy it equally. Porn gives a very one-sided view and, if it's believed, a very dangerous and unhappy one.

"Why are girls sometimes called slags and boys seen as studs? It's not fair."

Because the world we live in is still disgracefully unfair in the way it treats girls and boys, women and men, on a whole load of levels. (Not always in favour of boys, I must add.)

What can we do about it? Every time a girl is disrespected for the same type of activity a boy is respected for, make a noise about it. Don't stand for it. Boys, show that you can use your brains and identify injustice. Girls, if you need to, explain the injustice.

"I went quite far with a boy and now he's boasting about it and exaggerating what happened."

"I knocked him back and now he's saying I had sex with him."

112

Boasting and exaggerating about sexual behaviour is an old story. It's probably not going to go away. Girls do it, too, not just boys. If you and your good friends stand up against it, putting out the message, "How pathetic of you to lie", it might help. Just be as calm as possible, as proud as possible and as mature as possible.

Why not try and make your school one which doesn't stand for this sort of behaviour? Get together some girls and boys who think the behaviour is wrong, and plan a campaign to make everyone understand.

> "He/she took a photo secretly
> and has now put it online."

> "He/she took a photo and has threatened to put
> it online if I don't do what he/she asks."

This is one stress people your age have to face which your parents' generation never did. There are many stories of this happening and it's awful for the people involved. While I was researching this, I came across a forum where a woman was asking advice because her ex-boyfriend had some pictures of her and she thought he was planning to put them online. Some of the advice she was given was nuts and sometimes dangerous, including the suggestion that she steal the photos back – dangerous and also pointless, because there could be any number of digital copies.

This type of threat or behaviour is horrible, truly horrible, a form of abuse and bullying which has led to young people taking their own lives. But that is not the answer, it really isn't. If you find yourself threatened in this way, don't panic; tell an adult immediately, even if it feels embarrassing. It can be stopped.

I'll be talking about **Cyber-bullying** separately.

> "My boyfriend looks at porn and he wants me to do what he's seen online but I don't want to. Is there something wrong with me?"

As I said above, many boys watch online porn and end up thinking that's how sex is meant to be. Sadly, many girls think this, too. But it isn't supposed to be like that. It's supposed to be something you both want. And if there is a single thing you don't want to do, you don't have to do it and he must not make you. If he forces you, it's rape. If he just tries to persuade you, you have to think whether you want to carry on seeing him. It's about respect. It's about being a decent human.

> "The boys in my school behave disgustingly towards girls and I often feel threatened or upset. Why are they allowed to make comments about my figure or say what they want to do to me?"

114

Your school needs to deal with this. It is unacceptable. I suggest that a group of you – and I bet there are some boys who would join you – get together, make a list of some of the worst things that have happened and arrange to meet a teacher. Choose one of you who is good at speaking and explain, calmly and articulately, what kind of behaviour is going on and how it is hurting you all and interfering with your work and your life. The teacher should take it very seriously, and something should be done by the management of the school. If the teacher doesn't take it seriously, speak to another one. Stand no nonsense.

PRESSURE TO HAVE SEX

"Everyone talks about how they've had sex – I must be the only one who hasn't."

You aren't. A lot of people boast and exaggerate to make themselves look and feel better. Also, are you absolutely sure that "everyone" is saying they have? I bet lots of people are keeping quiet and you aren't even noticing. And, of the noisy ones, some are lying. Anyway, the important thing is that you do it when it's right for you and it doesn't matter whether you're 20, 25, 35 or any age. You should not do anything a moment before you really want to.

There is sexual pressure from all sides at your stage of life. Try to stay true to what you believe and want. Stick with people you respect, and do what genuinely feels right to you. Don't give in to pressure from people you don't really respect; value your self-esteem and that will keep you strong. And once you get through these years, it will be much easier to stick with people who have the same values as you and to avoid peer pressure.

"My boyfriend/girlfriend wants to go further than I'm ready for - I'm scared we'll split up if we don't do it."

This is a common worry and is not new, I promise. It's easy for me to give the usual answer: "If your boyfriend/ girlfriend really likes and respects you, he or she will wait until you are ready." But I know this doesn't help when you are in the turmoil of a relationship. All I can say is that if your boyfriend or girlfriend doesn't care for you enough to consider your wishes, it's perhaps not such a good relationship... Try to imagine what you'll feel like if you've done something you didn't really want to do.

"I don't want sex yet - is that normal?"

"How do I explain that I don't want to have sex?"

Just say so. And yes, it's normal. You should not feel pressured in any way to do anything any earlier than you want to. It is perfectly possible to have a fantastic relationship with a boyfriend or girlfriend and not have sex.

MAKING MISTAKES

"I went further than I wanted to
and now I regret it."

"I agreed to sex to please him/her
but I wish I hadn't."

There is no point in regretting this. It's done and can't be undone. In the grand scheme of your life this will not turn out to be a massively important issue, even if it seems major now. Try not to dwell on it. Use it as a learning experience and think how you will act the next time you are in the situation of deciding whether to have sex.

There is an exception to that advice and that is if you are from a culture which makes life extremely difficult (and dangerous) for girls when their families believe they have acted promiscuously. If you believe that you are at risk of violence, seek help. Your school should have someone who can advise. Or you can go to a health clinic for young people – see the resources section – because they will advise you confidentially and expertly. This is a more serious topic than I feel qualified to handle. But one thing I know: you should not have to live in fear and you need to tell someone if you are.

"I had unprotected sex and now
I'm terrified that I'm pregnant
or I've caught a disease."

Pregnancy

If you had unprotected sex within the last five days, there is what is usually called the "morning after pill". There are a few different sorts, some working three days and at least one working up to five days after sex, but they are more effective if taken within the first 12–24 hours.

How can you get it?

- GP appointment. Make sure the receptionist knows it's urgent. Treatment will be free and confidential.
- Local pharmacy. Depending on where you live and your age, you may have to pay. (Ask.)
- Access the internet and search "emergency contraception for young people" and add the first half of your postcode to find local services.

Sexually transmitted infections/diseases

STIs/STDs are transmitted when people have more than one partner. There is treatment for all of them, but if you leave an infection untreated, this can cause more serious problems later, including infertility. However, unlike worry about pregnancy, it is not an emergency if you are just worried about the risk from unprotected sex but don't have symptoms. If you have symptoms already (itchiness and discharge around the genitals) make a GP or clinic appointment as soon as possible, but definitely don't panic.

The most common infection is chlamydia, and it affects one in twelve young people aged sixteen to twenty-five in England. There is a simple test you can order online and do at home. The test is free in most parts of the UK. You need to wait about two weeks between having sex and doing the test, though. See the resources section for the website.

For any reassurance or testing for any sex-related worries, even if you have no symptoms at all, you can pop into your local free National Health Service clinic. (These are separate from your normal GP practice.) Every area of the UK has special health clinics and the staff will put you at your ease. You don't need to be embarrassed: they've seen everything and will not judge you. You don't have to be registered and they usually open in the evenings so you can go after school and no one needs to know.

You can go at any age and the clinic won't tell your parents. If they believe that you are in danger or need help, they may want to ask for other support, but they will discuss this with you first.

To find your local clinic, go onto the internet and search "young people's health" or "sexual health" or "sexually transmitted diseases" and add the first half of your postcode.

SEX WHEN YOU DIDN'T WANT IT

"What is date rape?"

"I didn't want sex and I said no but I didn't struggle. I can't explain why – I just shut my mind and let it happen."

"He didn't penetrate me but he made me do things to him that I didn't want to do."

If you didn't want sex but someone forces you (either physically or by physical threats) to perform a sexual act that you didn't want at the time when it was happening, this is rape. It is also rape if you were unable to give proper consent because you were drunk or drugged. So, it is rape if you made it clear that you didn't want it or if you were unable to communicate or understand what was happening.

Remember that you have the right to say no at any time.

"Date rape" is rape by someone who is not a stranger to you; perhaps you were on a date or seeing each other and the situation went further than you wanted. You must give clear signals that you don't want it but you can change your mind at any point. If you say no at any point, the other person must stop.

"I was drunk and really didn't know what I was doing. I would never have done it if I'd been sober."

"He got me drunk to make me say yes."

"Everyone was drunk and I know I had more than I meant to – I hardly remember what happened, to be honest."

This is tricky. The law says that if you are drunk you are not able to give free consent, so, technically, you did not consent. Therefore, it was rape. But what will happen will depend partly on how drunk you were, and that's usually very difficult to assess afterwards. I can't give you an expert view on the law but I suggest you talk to someone who can go into the details, because your relationship with the other person and your relative ages will make a difference to the situation.

"I think my drink was spiked but I can't prove it – I woke up and had no memory of how I'd got there but I think I had sex, even though I don't remember it."

121

You may have heard about "date rape" drugs like Rohypnol (roofies/rufies), GHB and ketamine. Drugs like these can easily be mixed in drinks to make someone black out and not know what is happening, and forget everything afterwards. Unfortunately, it can be hard to prove unless you get medical help within twenty-four hours. If you suspect that this has happened to you, tell a responsible adult immediately.

If you have been raped, or think you have but are not sure, or you don't exactly know whether what happened to you counts as rape:

- Call or find a friend, family member or someone you feel safe with and tell them what happened.
- Call a rape crisis centre. There is a web address and phone number at the back of this book. They will give you all the advice and support you need.
- If you're hurt, go straight to a hospital accident and emergency department.
- If you want to report the rape, call the police right away. Don't change clothes or wash, even though you will desperately want to. A trained doctor will examine you and make you feel as comfortable and safe as possible.
- Occasionally a woman or girl makes a false rape accusation. They do it because they are upset, or

ashamed, scared, angry or any number of strong emotional reasons. Later, perhaps they want to own up but it's hard to stop once you've started telling a story. Please be brave and tell the truth. To make a false rape accusation will not help you and it will devastate and destroy the person you accuse. If you are overwhelmed with anger or fear, take steps to deal with that, but don't lash out in a way that will ultimately hurt you. Talk to a good friend and work out what to do about whatever has upset you or whatever awful situation you're in.

- If you have already made a false accusation, be brave and own up as soon as possible. At an early stage, it can be dealt with much more simply and sympathetically; once the case has reached the court process, it's far more difficult and there's a chance of being prosecuted yourself. So, tell a responsible adult – parent, teacher, social worker, doctor, youth worker. Owning up is massively difficult but you must do it and, eventually, you will feel better, knowing you did the right thing. Almost nothing is as bad as worrying about it.

"Girls sometimes dress incredibly tartily and sexily – how can they expect boys to understand if they don't want sex?"

"I thought she wanted it. She seemed to at first,
then she changed her mind but it was too late."

You might *think* that dressing or behaving sexily means a
girl is "up for it". Many grown men think that, too. Wrongly.
Anyone may dress how they like (as long as they're not
breaking the law of the country they're in). Get used to
it! Sex should always be something that two people want
and that they are legally and physically able to consent to.

I think both boys/men and girls/women need to
understand that they have a lot of power over each other
and accept that with that power comes responsibility. Mis-
understandings happen, feelings get out of control, but
growing up is partly about learning our boundaries,
learning to respect ourselves and each other. It's one of
the reasons why there is a legal age of consent, because
the law recognises that younger people find self-control a
lot harder. Unfortunately, many adults haven't mastered it
either.

No one should abuse their power over another person. The stronger partner has an extra duty to ensure that
consent is freely given.

"I'm sixteen but my girlfriend is fifteen
– do we have to wait?"

According to the law of the country you are in, you must

wait until both of you are above the age of consent, which is sixteen in the UK but not in all countries. Otherwise you will be guilty of "unlawfully having sex with a minor", which is sometimes called "statutory rape". Even if your girlfriend wants to have sex, the law considers her not able to make that decision. You may disagree with the law but breaking it could have enormous consequences.

So it's not just your girlfriend who is breaking the law if she is under age, but you, too, even though you are sixteen. However, if you are in a relationship and if both partners are similar in age (usually defined as being not more than three years apart) and if the older partner is not in a position of authority (such as being a teacher or coach), many countries, including the UK and US, may use something called Romeo and Juliet laws, which look at these situations sympathetically and simply try to make sure that the younger person is safe. This means that although you are still breaking the law if your partner is under age, the chances are fairly good that you will not be treated as a criminal and you are unlikely to be accused of rape, unless it obviously was. However, you can't be sure about this and there have been cases of a young person being put on the sex offenders register even in a consenting relationship. The law is there for the protection of everybody but it is humans who administer the law and not all humans in authority behave as kindly or sympathetically as others.

NOT HAVING A BOYFRIEND OR GIRLFRIEND

"No one ever fancies me!"

"I've never had a boy/girlfriend – I'm obsessing about it."

"When my friend and I go anywhere, people are always hitting on her/him, never me."

Being "fancied" by lots of people has very little to do with straightforward "good looks" or prettiness. Someone incredibly attractive can look intimidating to more averagely good-looking people. Or maybe people just give off different vibes. Whatever the truth, it's pretty hard to do anything about that and, to be honest, I don't think you should, other than relaxing about it.

I know it's hard not to obsess, but relationships happen when they happen and not when you go looking for them. On the other hand, it's worth pointing out that you need to meet people if you want a relationship, so joining clubs and doing activities outside school will make it more likely. Just don't think about it too much.

"My relationships only ever last a couple of weeks. Is something wrong with me?"

That was me, actually – until eventually I met the right person, and then it worked. Nothing is "wrong" with you. Everyone has different things they want from a relationship; some people are fussier than others. Let's call it having high standards. High standards are good.

I can't say whether you'll fall in love sooner or later but I do know there's absolutely no point in stressing about it now. Enjoy your life, your friends and all the opportunities that come your way. And you might just come across someone you really hit it off with. You can't force it to happen. It happens by chance, and often when you aren't looking for it.

Besides, having lots of less serious relationships at your age is fine, too. You're still changing and working out who you are, so it's pretty understandable that so many relationships don't last very long.

SUGGESTED STRATEGIES
AND THINGS TO THINK ABOUT:

- Just be yourself, be patient, don't go out of your way to attract anyone, but make sure you go to places where other teenagers are, because staying in your room is not going to work.

- If you're obsessing about it, find things to take your mind off the topic. Hang out with friends, make new friends, try a new hobby. All those things not only take your mind off the fact that

127

you want a boyfriend or girlfriend, they also make it more likely that you'll find one.

- There are lots of advantages to not having a boyfriend/girlfriend! You can spend time with friends, you can have fun without pressure, you can have more control over what you do and you won't constantly have to think, "Does he/she really fancy me?" You also won't have to go through the heartache of breaking up... I know that's not much consolation but I'm encouraging you not to waste the next few months worrying about something that will almost certainly sort itself out, usually when you least expect it.

- Ask your parents or other adults where they met the person they ended up in a relationship with. It's amazing how many relationships started by pure chance.

"Not having a boyfriend/girlfriend gives you freedom to be yourself – embrace it."

Kathryn, adult

BREAKING UP

"I've just broken up with someone and I can't get over it – I think about him/her all the time."

"I can't go into school because my ex-boyfriend and his mates will all laugh at me."

"She dumped me a week before exams – and now I can't work at all. It's going to ruin my life!"

Breaking up is horrible whatever your age. When you're a teenager the emotions are new and raw. And sometimes it's very public because people at school will know. But nearly everyone who has ever been in love has also broken up.

SUGGESTED STRATEGIES
AND THINGS TO THINK ABOUT:

- Scientists have shown that the brain areas that are active when we are rejected are the same as those that are active when we suffer physical pain. So don't be surprised if the symptoms really do feel physical. You're not over-reacting or being silly, and they *will* fade, just like the symptoms of physical pain. I promise.

- It's tough going into school or seeing your friends when you've just broken up with someone. All I can do is encourage you to be brave and face it early, because that first day is going to be the difficult one. It will get easier after that. Also, ask a good friend to stick with you and give you moral support.

- If it happens just before an exam, or during exams, this obviously puts huge extra pressure on you and it may be really hard to put the pain aside and focus. The best thing to do is to channel your emotion into producing adrenalin for the exam. If you are feeling angry or sad or confused, channel those feelings into doing the very best you possibly can in this exam. Later, when it's over, then you can let go of the emotions and cry or shout or whatever, but you'll have the satisfaction of knowing that you did your best and nothing could rock you.

- It's normal to feel really powerful emotions at first but if these emotions don't fade after a few weeks, you may need to talk to someone who can help you change your thought patterns.

"What stresses me most is when my ex-girlfriend tries to speak to me."

Chris, 16

LGBT (LESBIAN, GAY, BISEXUAL AND TRANSGENDER)

Not everyone is attracted to the opposite sex (hetero-sexual). It's a plain fact. It should be no one's business but the individuals concerned and should not affect anyone else. Many people of my generation realized when they were teenagers that they didn't fancy people of the opposite sex, and very many of them didn't know what to do about it or how to deal with it in a world which was very hostile to homosexuality. (It still is in some places and in some parts of society.) Even though there's now much greater understanding of and respect for gay people in the UK and elsewhere, "coming out" is still often difficult.

It's also true that during your early teenage years you may genuinely not be sure whether you are heterosexual, homosexual or bisexual (attracted to people of either gender). Many teenagers, however, are quite certain, even from an early age.

What you need first is to be able to talk about it to people (or even just one person) who will understand and who will like and respect you as they did before. They can help you tell everyone else and soon you'll be able simply to be yourself.

You'll find resources at the back of this book: a website where you can communicate with others who have dealt with exactly the same worries, decisions and situations.

You might take comfort from the fact that most teenagers are going through some kind of stress to do with relationships and sexual attraction so you're not alone in being confused and overwhelmed by your feelings. Finding people who support you and who understand you is your main goal in dealing with your worries.

A word about parents: all parents are different but there is something I'd like you to think about, especially if your parents react badly or seem upset when you tell them. (Many parents react well, by the way, and often say they'd always known and were just waiting for you to say something.) If it comes as a huge surprise, your parents may suddenly see you as a different person, though actually you are just the same. You see, they may well have assumed that you would probably one day have children. Parents are, in some ways, programmed by biology to think about having grandchildren eventually. You may think that's ridiculous and none of their business, but I'm just giving you an insight into how they might feel. Clearly, they have to get over it. If you're gay, you're gay, and they have to deal with it. But for some parents it's hard. It is not surprising if you are angry with them for not understanding or respecting you, but you may need to give them time.

Some religious faiths may also make it harder but all I can say is that, in my view, a good person puts humanity and biological reality before a religious rule.

Most parents and other relatives will soon get used to you being different from how they expected. And they will (or should) quickly realize that how you are is how you are and that inside you are exactly the same person as before. Except that no one is exactly the same as they were a year ago, or two years ago – you are growing up, and the adults around you have to deal with that.

> *"My biggest stress as a teenager is body dysphoria and people who knowingly misgender me."*
> **Taylor, 16**

Transgender issues

What if you are one of those people who does not feel that he or she is the "right" gender? Perhaps you feel that you are in the wrong body, that you were "supposed" to be the opposite gender to the body you've been born with. This is not just wishing you'd been born a boy or girl, but actually feeling that, inside, you *are* the opposite gender.

If this is a new feeling, I recommend you wait and see how you feel in some months. It's very possible that this is part of the general confusion and upheaval of hormones. If the feeling doesn't go away or if it's one you've had for some years, I suggest you talk to an expert because there is a great deal of good advice they can give you. You could start by talking to your doctor or someone at one of the young people's health clinics that most areas in the UK have, where you can get free, confidential advice.

Adults and families

Some of you live with two parents, some with one; some have step-parents or foster parents or carers, or you may be in care. It's hard to cover each of these separately so I'm just going to refer to "your adults".

I am also very aware that although some young people have very supportive families (though there may still be arguments), others live in really difficult situations and may have no support at all. I want this book to be able to help all of you, whatever type of home you have, but I know some of what I say won't apply to everyone or may seem to ignore certain people. I'm really sorry. Please just find the bits that you need and see the resources at the end for further help.

If you have severe difficulties at home, especially if you feel that the situation is harmful to you, or frightening, please get proper help. No one should have to put up with fear or real unhappiness, and there's all sorts of help for you. A good starting point is usually your school, which should have a guidance department with teachers trained to be confidential, sympathetic and wise, and to know where to get more help for you if necessary.

One important point for adults and teenagers to remember is that this is all about moving towards independence. If you are to become a fully independent adult with your own opinions, it's natural that there should be some breaking away from the adults who have been looking after you. This can be stressful at the time but it helps if you and they see it as positive. Those relationships can become good again later, once you're independent.

Let's look at some of the problems you may have with the people you live with.

"They look at me as though I'm an alien.
I think they're the aliens."

"They never listen to my opinions."

"Everyone seems to want to stop me
doing what I want."

"They say 'grow up' but they treat me like a child."

This is probably the most common set of complaints teenagers have about their adults. I don't think it has changed much in a hundred years.

SUGGESTED STRATEGIES
AND THINGS TO THINK ABOUT:

● They probably *don't* understand you. Until a few years ago, scientists didn't know as much as they know now about the brain and how physical brain changes can affect teenagers. Most adults still don't know much about it. So, you could get them to look at my website, where they will find lots of information about the teenage brain.

● Most teenagers feel like this at least some of the time. Remember that you are moving away from being a child and towards being an adult but it doesn't happen straightaway; and it's often very hard for adults to let go of the control they had when you were younger.

● Also – you won't like me saying this, but it's true – while you want to do certain things and you believe you can, sometimes you aren't ready. Now, you may say that your adults have to let you take risks and make your own mistakes, and that's true to an extent, but it's also their job to protect you from unnecessary risk or danger. The balance and struggle between those two things is hard, for you and for your adults. This often means conflict.

● Try to think of this conflict as merely irritating and temporary. And do everything you can to show your adults how responsible and brilliant you are; then they are more likely to trust you.

● In some ways, many parents never 100% let go. It's really, really hard, and we never stop worrying. Ask my daughters – who are in their twenties! I do my best not to interfere, but...

"Hang on in there. One day you will understand why adults are pains in the necks. It's not because they don't understand how you feel. They understand only too well. It's just that teenagers and adults often speak different languages."
Sally, adult

"Inwardly I was very insecure. Outwardly I was indestructible. I would never listen to adults and subsequently I sometimes got myself into situations I could easily have avoided. I thought I knew everything, and I thought I was very mature. I also thought that everything I did was forever – such as friendships, decisions I made and things that were said to me. Other people's opinions of me were SO very important. They shaped my self-esteem (which should probably be called someone-else's-esteem)."
Christine, adult

"They don't give me any freedom and I'm being left out of things my friends do."

"They're stricter than anyone else."

It's very common to think that your adults are stricter than anyone else's. It might be true but it might not be.

SUGGESTED STRATEGIES
AND THINGS TO THINK ABOUT:

- In general, adults make rules because they care and they worry.
- Sometimes, the rules they make are right. (Sorry.) Often it's really hard for parents to set rules, especially when other parents don't, but they do it because they care.
- Sometimes, parents get it wrong because they have misjudged the risks. In this case, try some calm negotiating tactics. Wait till they are not busy or stressed or angry and say you want to talk about whatever it is. There is an art to handling parents and you'll make life a whole lot better if you learn how.
- Negotiating boundaries requires skill. Adults are supposed to set boundaries to protect you. Sometimes they set wrong boundaries, too tight or too wide. If you can explain, calmly and rationally, why a boundary should be different, do

so. Avoid doing that eye-rolling thing; it's likely to make adults dig their heels in and not want to negotiate. Being stroppy and shouting doesn't work nearly as well as being calm and rational.

⊙ Another way to encourage adults to relax strict boundaries is by demonstrating that you can be trusted. This doesn't always work and requires patience. And you may need to point out that you've just *done* something trustworthy. Parents don't always notice.

SECTION TWO

"I get on really badly with them – I actually hate them."

"I can't talk to them about anything – I don't respect them at all."

Was it always like this or is it just since you became a teenager? If it was always like this, I suspect it's not likely to get better during the teenage years. If it's become much worse recently or only started during adolescence, there are two possible reasons: either your adults have something stressful going on in *their* lives or they're finding your teenage behaviour hard to understand and manage. They may be right or they may be over-reacting.

It may be that you're *right* not to respect your parents. Some adults are pretty rubbish. Many are also struggling with a whole load of their own problems and may not be able to look past them to see yours. This is not something to be proud of but adults make mistakes and mess up, because they're human.

SUGGESTED STRATEGIES
AND THINGS TO THINK ABOUT:

- If you think your parents are behaving unreasonably, why don't you try showing them that you can be more "adult" than them? Try a charm offensive, by doing some housework or offering to cook a meal or mow the lawn.

- Is there something difficult going on in their lives that you could sympathise with? They will really appreciate that and it could make a huge difference.

- Be patient – this could just be a phase, while they get used to the fact that you aren't a child.

- Let them know, choosing a good and quiet moment, that you need their help. Showing someone that you're really upset can be helpful, but anger tends not to work. Communication can be so difficult when relationships are strained but if you can possibly find a way it will be really helpful.

- Make them learn about what is going on in your brain and body. Understanding reasons for things can have a hugely positive effect. (My website will help them.)

● Hate is a common emotion, so don't feel guilty about it. However, it's also a very negative one and won't help either you or them.

● If your relationship with your adults is genuinely a nightmare, look ahead to a time when you will be independent. Maybe, when you are an adult, you'll find a better relationship with them.

● Don't let it ruin your life. It's only one part of your daily existence. I know it's an important part and it may really be getting you down, but focus on making the rest of your life – school and friends – work well for you, so that one day you can show your parents what a great person you are.

● Try some of the relaxation techniques in *SECTION THREE*; it's likely that you are very stressed and this can't be helping your relationships at home.

"I've got no one – I'm on my own."

"They're in prison/alcoholics/drug addicts – they can't help me."

You are not alone: there are many young people in your situation. But it's really tough and you deserve better. Trouble is, life isn't fair. Many teenagers manage to rise above their very difficult start in life and achieve great things. But you need strength and you need help.

Luckily there is help out there for you, whatever your specific problem. You will find detailed resources at the back of this book, but here's some general advice.

SUGGESTED STRATEGIES
AND THINGS TO THINK ABOUT:

- Friends are vital but make sure they're the right friends. You need good influences, steady people who can listen and be calm for you.

- Although you need help, the strength also needs to come from inside. Charities and the State are there to help you, but they can't if you don't help yourself. Believe in yourself. Sometimes you will make mistakes, but don't give up.

- Just because your adults have given you a really bad start doesn't mean you have to behave like them. You don't inherit badness in your genes; yes, it's not easy overcoming a negative environment, but it's possible. It may be hard now, as a teenager, but when you're an adult you'll find extra strength.

- Don't blame yourself for what has happened. And don't waste energy blaming your parents.

- Go to any teacher you like or trust and ask for help; if that teacher can't help, she or he can direct you towards the best person.

- Is there another adult you trust? Just to talk to. A relative or friend or parent of a friend?
- Don't despair about the future: you can change it, maybe just not yet.
- Do your best. That's all anyone can expect. Be proud of everything you achieve. If you are do-ing it without support at home, be extra proud.

YOUNG CARERS

"I am a carer for my mum/dad."

"I spend so much time helping my parents that I have no time to be with friends – and my work is falling behind."

Is your school aware of your situation? According to the website of Barnardo's, which does special work to help young carers, among the 175,000 young carers in the UK, 13,000 care for more than fifty hours a week. They also say that the average age of a young carer is twelve, and that very many young carers have the added challenges of living in one-parent families or caring for someone with mental health problems.

If you are one of these young people, first, you are remarkable and should be very proud. Second, if you

143

need help, you deserve it and should ask for it. The person you care for is important and special to you but you are important and special too. If you don't need help, fine, but if you do, don't be too proud to ask. There are some resources at the end of the book, including a blog by young-adult carers. If none of these resources helps you, please tell someone at your school, or a social worker, that you want help.

SEPARATION/DIVORCE/CONFLICT

"My parents are getting divorced."

"My parents are always fighting – I'm worried they are getting divorced."

"It feels like my fault that they argue – they seem angry with me all the time."

It's not your fault if your parents are splitting up: they are adults and it's down to something that's gone wrong between them and not you. They may seem to be using you as a way to get at each other, which they wouldn't want to do if they were thinking clearly. But they are angry and stressed themselves and may not be noticing how you are feeling. People under emotional strain don't behave as they normally would.

"The things that stress me most are the effects of my mother and father being divorced; it stresses me out as they always argue about silly things."

Michaela, 16

SUGGESTED STRATEGIES
AND THINGS TO THINK ABOUT:

- Parents often argue and go through bad patches; it doesn't necessarily mean they are going to get divorced.

- If they do, it might be better. It won't be nice at first but things often calm down and families find a way to live separately. It is estimated that just over 40% of UK marriages end in divorce, so you are definitely not alone.

- If you think they're ignoring your needs, remind them how you are feeling. There are many on-line resources for parents going through divorce.

- Although you care about them, their happiness is not your responsibility. Adults need to sort this out. Think of yourself first.

- Read novels about people of your age dealing with divorce; each situation will be different but it will help you get perspective. Try your school or local library.

Problems with step-families

According to the organisation Care for the Family, a third of the UK population is part of a step-family in some way.

Having a step-family can be incredibly difficult, especially at first. In fact, it's pretty rare for it not to be worrying and stressful in the early stages. Often, it ends up being far better than you could have imagined, but sometimes it doesn't. Certainly, how it is at first will not be how it is a few months later, and the most difficult part will usually be those first weeks and months.

Because everyone knows how difficult it is, there are lots of organisations and resources designed to help, both online and as books, including novels. And because it's so common, it's almost certain that you will know someone who has been through the experience of meeting a new step-family, so you probably have a friend you can talk to about it.

Your parents will want it to go smoothly, too. Adults should try very hard to make it as easy as possible for you, because the fact that they split up in the first place is not your fault. However, adults going through break-ups or starting with a new partner often don't see things clearly, and might not understand what you're thinking or feeling. Sometimes it's up to you to point it out.

SUGGESTED STRATEGIES
AND THINGS TO THINK ABOUT:

- Remember that no one will find this easy, so if you find it hard, you are not alone.

- Your position in the family may change. If you were the oldest, perhaps you now won't be. Or if you were the only girl, maybe now you aren't. It'll be difficult at first but should get better, if you all try hard. But some people don't try hard, I'm afraid. All you can do is make sure *you* do.

- It's almost certain that jealousies will arise. Accept this as natural.

- If your own parent or parents seem to be neglecting you and focusing on their new partner, this is very normal. It is not because they don't love you. It's because they are wrapped up in their own new emotions. It can be really annoying (and worrying) for you so I suggest some gentle reminders that you exist, you are hurting and you need some attention.

- Talk to your friends.

- Be patient. Be strong. Be brave. Focus on the things you can change and not the things you can't. And when other people are behaving badly, keep behaving well. Then you'll feel good about yourself, and feeling good about yourself is very, very important when it comes to stress.

147

Problems with brothers and sisters

Because you are changing so fast, your relationship with brothers and sisters can change, too, and you may find them incredibly irritating. Even more irritating than before, if that's possible. They may also find you incredibly irritating, to be fair. Your relationship with them will depend on lots of things. For example, your personalities, and whether they are younger than you or older and how close in age. Relationships will also be affected by other things going on in your family life that none of you may be able to control: such as illness, divorce, money worries, and many other things that can stop family life being smooth. And how difficult you are finding your teenage years will also make a difference.

SUGGESTED STRATEGIES
AND THINGS TO THINK ABOUT:

● Don't get too hung up on problems with brothers and sisters. It's so normal. And everything
will change when you're all older. Of course, that
doesn't mean that all the problems necessarily
go away. Many brothers and sisters just don't get
on well, but it should become less important as
you find your own lives later on. There's a saying:
"You can choose your friends but you can't
choose your family." You do not have to be best
friends with your brothers or sisters.

148

● But don't wreck your own happiness or make life more stressful for yourself by allowing more arguments to happen than necessary. If your brothers or sisters annoy you, try to keep out of their way. Don't annoy them back as this very rarely makes things better for you.

Bullying and Cyber-bullying

Unfortunately, bullying happens at any age, including sometimes amongst adults. People can be cruel, thoughtless and ignorant. Sometimes bullies don't even know they are hurting their targets. Sometimes they do know, and it's awful to realize there are people who would deliberately and knowingly hurt someone else. But sometimes those people are also hurting; they may have horrible things happening at home, things that have made them behave in ugly ways.

If you are being bullied, I don't suppose you feel sympathy for the bully, and I don't blame you, because being bullied is terrible. It can also be physically frightening and the bullying can be violent. It can drive people to despair and even, in extreme circumstances, suicide. Please, if you are thinking about this even for a minute, get help. That is not the answer to bullying. Never. There are other solutions, but it can be very difficult to see them when you are going through it.

According to research for the government in 2009, almost half of all UK children (46%) say they have been bullied at some point. Most of the young people who responded said their school dealt with it pretty well. If you think yours doesn't, tell them.

"If you're being bullied, talk about it. I wish I had. If you're bullying someone, you could be scarring that person for life. Don't be fooled by apparent indifference. Inside, it hurts."

Miriam, adult

What is bullying?

Bullying can take many forms. It can be name-calling, making up lies about you, minor physical things such as pinching or pushing, stealing or damaging your possessions, saying nasty things about you behind your back or on the internet, threatening you, sending offensive texts or making offensive or silent phone calls.

Bullying can be racist or sexist; it can be aimed at criticising your body; it can be because you are cleverer or better in some way than the bullies; it can also be aimed at any disabilities or differences you might have.

How is this different for teenagers? The things that can happen are the same, and the feelings are the same whatever your age, but there are a few differences and extra points to make.

- The bullying may have a sexual element. I've heard of schools where the girls regularly feel threatened by boys. The examples may seem minor: things like name-calling or bra-pinging or comments about periods. But those things are not minor; they may make girls feel they can't be themselves, that their changing bodies are under scrutiny by boys. Boys are sometimes the targets of equivalent teasing. Just at the age when you're very self-conscious about your body, you should not be made to feel worse about it. Some sexual bullying goes much, much further than this and can even involve sexual assault.

- Problems can arise when boyfriend/girlfriend relationships end. It can add an extra dimension and cruelty to the bullying, especially when it happens online.

- You may feel less able to tell your parents or a teacher, especially if there's a sexual element to it.

- A great deal of teenage bullying is made worse by the cruel and dangerous use of social media, such as Facebook and online messaging. This is so important that there is a whole section on it. (See **Cyber-bullying**.)

SUGGESTED STRATEGIES
AND THINGS TO THINK ABOUT:

- Don't let bullies get away with it. With "minor" examples, you might just ignore them, but if it doesn't stop, or it gets worse, don't suffer in silence. Schools must deal with bullies, so speak to a teacher if the bullies go to your school or another school you know. This will be confidential and the school must find a way not to put you at greater risk. You might speak to your guidance teacher, head of year or school librarian. You might put it in writing, if you don't want to say it out loud.

- Try to tell your parents or carers. The bullies don't want you to tell anyone so they will want to frighten you into silence. Don't let them.

- If you are physically attacked or threatened, this is assault and it's a crime. It is now even more important to tell an adult you trust. Please.

- Keep a record of the bullying, with dates. This is very useful for any adult trying to sort out the situation. Note what happened and how you felt.

- If possible, avoid being on your own. There is strength in numbers and it is also useful if some-one witnesses any threats or signs of bullying.

- Don't fight back with violence.

- Never blame yourself if you are bullied. Bullies

bully whoever they want and it's not your fault. Yes, there are certain types of people who are more often bullied, usually people who are not like the bullies. For example, people who ask questions in class, or who are serious and get on with their work. Sometimes there's no reason at all but the bullies just think they will have fun bullying you.

● Talk to your friends. Friends will understand. Otherwise they aren't friends.

● Focus on the things at school and home that make you happy, whether it's a hobby, sport, or just hanging out with friends. Hold onto your friends: they are more important than the bullies.

● Learn self-defence or a martial art. Not to fight back but to feel more confident and defend yourself. Often, when the bullies see that you can defend yourself, they will stop, because they are cowards.

● Never, ever let bullies stop you doing well at the things you are good at. Aim for a glittering future – that's the best way of defeating them.

● Start an anti-bullying campaign in your school or area. Alex Holmes did this, creating anti-bullying ambassadors in his school and helping himself and others. (This is described in the InspireMyKids website at the back of this book, along with other useful websites.)

Talking about glittering futures, there are many stories of young people who were badly bullied at school going on to have enormous success. To me, this sounds a bit obvious, because we know that people with all sorts of skills and value are bullied. I'm making the point because being bullied can make you feel ugly, stupid and worthless. It can make you feel that life is not worth living. Life is worth living. It is. You can overcome this and move on.

Are you a bully?

I hope not. If you are, I hope you'd like to stop. Bullies are weak people pretending to be strong. Think how much better it would be if you could focus on your own life, your own talents, your own hopes and dreams.

You may be bullying because you are going along with what your "friends" do. The really brave, big thing to do is find different friends. Before it's too late and you get yourself into major trouble, trouble that will make you feel bad about yourself and may damage your future.

If you feel guilty because you've been bullying some-one, now is a good time to make a fresh start. Everyone makes mistakes and does the wrong thing sometimes. Now you can undo some of the damage. A genuine apology and a promise never to do it again will really help the person you victimised.

Cyber-bullying

Cyber-bullying is any bullying that takes place online or using mobile phones – in other words, not face to face. The fact that it's not face to face can make the bullies do and say even worse things than in other sorts of bullying. It gives cowards extra power; it means that the bullying takes place at any time of day or night; and it can be very public.

Often, the bullies don't even think it's bullying. Not seeing a victim's reaction makes them braver and more thoughtless.

Cyber-bullying includes: sending nasty text messages and emails; abuse on social media; spreading lies on blogs, social media or websites; setting up hate blogs or websites aimed at the target or pretending to be written by the target; and posting and spreading photographs (often of a sexual nature). If you become the victim of any of these things – and very many young people are – it will make you feel sick, scared and horrified.

You probably already know the rules about keeping safe online. This book isn't the place to go into them because this is about how to deal with the stress if it actually happens to you, but there are some resources at the back.

Apparently, fewer than 20% of young people report what has happened or tell their parents. Yet the main advice that all experts give is to report it. Talk to someone even if you believe they can't do anything. There is so often an easier solution than you imagine.

POSTING IMAGES: THE LAW

It is illegal to post a picture of a sexual nature, even if the person consented and even if the person is over sixteen. Anyone who then re-posts that picture is also committing a criminal offence.

If the image is of someone under sixteen, it's even more serious. Someone under sixteen cannot, legally, "consent", and it is illegal to post online or publish in any way any sexual image of someone under sixteen. Even if it's of yourself. Also, forwarding, downloading or re-posting such an image is an offence.

All this is important for two main reasons:

1. Many people don't realize that passing on a picture created by someone else is not just "a bit of a joke". It's against the law and can lead to a criminal record.

2. Also, if someone threatens to put a sexual picture or video of you online (or anywhere where someone might see it), the fact that it's a crime gives you and the people who care for you a

156

useful weapon to stop it happening. The bully
probably doesn't realize what a serious crime
it is and when they do they may stop. They are,
remember, cowards.

So, it's important for both bullies (or people thinking
of bullying) and victims to understand how serious
the law on this is. It can mean someone ending up on
the sex offenders register.

"What can I do to stop the online bullying?
It's making my life hell."

Whatever the type of online bullying, it creates feelings
of powerlessness, fear and an overwhelming stress that
affects you day and night. You need help and there is lots
of help for you.

And remember my points above about the law: this
should give you strong protection, if used well. However,
don't take the law into your own hands. Trusted adults are
the right people to help.

SUGGESTED STRATEGIES
AND THINGS TO THINK ABOUT:

● Report it. Immediately. Even if you are embarrassed. Tell a trusted adult. Parents may not be

157

experts but they can find experts who will help you in practical ways.

- Never reply to bullying messages and do not comment on any blog or website where you find yourself or anyone else being abused. Replying to hate online is called "feeding trolls" and you should not feed trolls (people who deliberately post offensive messages) because that's what they want. They like it because they know they've hurt you. (Horrible, I know, but then bullying is horrible.)

- Don't take matters into your own hands. Just report it and let adults take over.

- Follow the advice on websites such as Kidscape, the anti-bullying site.

- Contact Childline for totally confidential, expert advice, especially if you have no one else to go to.

- Block the people doing it from all your sites. Change your passwords.

- Keep evidence. Take screenshots and record phone calls. If you don't know how to do this, look it up online – maybe with a friend – referring to the device you use.

- If you think you have given away personal information that has exposed you, tell a trusted adult, even before something bad happens.

- If you think someone has an embarrassing photo of you, remember that no one has the right to post it anywhere and they may be committing a crime if they do. Tell them it would be a crime. If that doesn't help, tell an adult. I know it's really difficult, but it's the best thing to do.
- Spreading lies about you is a crime if it hurts you, including psychologically. The police deal with crimes, so you or any adult can contact the police. However, I recommend contacting the school first.
- You are not alone and none of this is your fault.
- Do not believe the comments about you – they are designed to hurt, not to be true.
- Never go to meet an online bully and never do anything they say.
- If anything happens to you online which you are even slightly uncomfortable about, tell someone.

All of the above advice centres around one thing: tell someone. So, tell someone! The best weapon is openness.

As with bullying, your school should be making all students aware of the dangers of online activity. If you don't think they're doing this well, speak to a teacher, on your own or with friends, to get them to improve their policy.

An extra point about schools

As I was writing this, a mother contacted me and said she'd phoned the school to discuss her concern about something happening to her daughter online and no one had phoned back. Many more people then contacted me, saying that their school had dodged the issue. Sometimes the excuse was that cyber-bullying happens outside school and therefore is not a school problem and another common reaction was that "all kids do it". All kids do not do it! Whoever is doing it needs to be shown that it is wrong, cruel, dangerous and nasty.

Schools are under pressure from all sides and they can't always take responsibility for things happening outside. However, if people from your school are harassing and bullying you in school or out of it, this will be affecting your education directly and your school needs to be involved.

I also came across many stories of excellent work by schools, and had many positive conversations with teachers responsible for child protection in their schools. Adults really do care and are worried about it; it's just that some have found better ways of dealing with it than others. I think a useful message is: if your school does a good job dealing with bullying, great; if it doesn't, don't just accept it. You have more power than you think.

"I surveyed my Year Sevens shortly after Christmas (206 students). On average in a class of tewnty-eight, about twelve had internet-capable smart phones. Of these NONE had been checked for security settings by parents. On average of the twelve, about seven students had active Facebook accounts – despite it being in breach of Facebook policy. The parents were not aware. THIS IS THE ROOT OF THE DANGER – IGNORANCE. And it is getting worse."

Secondary school CEOP coordinator

"I wish they would ban phones and iPods from school, I really do. We have had issues with Facebook, Instagram and LiveProfile, not to mention BlackBerry Messenger, where both of my daughters' accounts were hacked by so-called friends."

Parent

"If teenagers are being bullied by these forms of media then they should make the media work for them. Record conversations on their phones. Keep copies of all texts and Facebook messages and hand them over to the school. They should also learn not to respond. By retaliating instantly, they often make the situation worse as tempers flare."

Two 13-year-olds who have been bullied on social media

"Collect/keep evidence. Discuss it tactfully and openly with your child. Make sure they know you believe them and offer them support. Talk to them about what actions could be taken. Talk to the police if applicable/appropriate. Reassure them. Help them find out what their school policy is and talk to someone trustworthy there."

Parent whose daughter was bullied online

Social Media and Phones

Mobile phones and social media sites can be great for making friends and having fun online. The new online world is wonderful and it means you can share your life with people all around the globe. It means you know more, are more open-minded, and more politically-aware than my generation ever was.

You know many of the dangers, too, and not just the problems of online bullying. By the time you are in secondary school, you'll have had loads of talks and instructions about how to use the internet safely. The trouble is that even adults get themselves tangled up in problems online and no one of any age can afford to be careless.

Also, new sites and social media platforms are springing up all the time. When I was researching for this chapter, I came across sites I'd never heard of before. Each has different risks and all of us, of any age, need to be very careful about all of them.

Let's look at some different sets of worries.

"I don't actually really like Facebook and those things but I get sucked into it because I don't want to miss out."

"I end up not getting my homework done because

I'm getting messages or I keep wanting
to check what's going on."

"I plan just to go on it for a couple of minutes
but an hour later..."

You have my sympathies with this. While I'm working I find it's all too easy to waste time looking at websites or reading and replying to messages from friends. I've found ways to ignore them so that I do get my work done, but it's not easy – and it may be harder for you, because for teenagers the urge not to miss out on anything is stronger.

SUGGESTED STRATEGIES
AND THINGS TO THINK ABOUT:

- Going online is very addictive. It quickly becomes a habit. Try to break the habit a bit at a time and see how good it makes you feel.
- Make a pact with a friend that you won't go on the internet for a certain amount of time.
- Switch your phone OFF while working. Always.
- If you are not actually using the internet for a piece of work, don't have it open. Certainly stay logged out of things like Facebook. If you find it too tempting, there are pieces of software that will block you from social media or the internet for certain periods of time.
- Some people find rules helpful. Write a rule on

a piece of paper and stick it above your desk. It could be: "Do forty minutes work and then go on the internet for ten minutes." Or: "Finish my homework before going on the internet." Whatever works for you.

● Remember: if you don't go on Facebook for two hours, everything will still be there when you do. It will probably be even more interesting if you wait!

You might like to know that a few days after writing that, I was having real trouble concentrating on work. I kept zapping between emails, Facebook, blog, Twitter, Facebook, blog, Twitter, emails. The fact that I couldn't concentrate was really annoying me. So, after lunch, as I was walking back to my office I decided to write myself a timetable for the afternoon. Seeing it written down made it seem manageable and positive, and sticking to it was easier.

"My parents have banned me from using the internet after 9 p.m. and they make me put my phone downstairs – it's so unfair!"

I like your parents already. There are several reasons why having electronic devices switched on in your bedroom during the hour or so before you go to bed is a bad idea.

I'll give more detail in **Sleep** but here is the outline.

First, the light from a backlit screen (all computers, phones, tablets etc, as well as televisions) will encourage your brain to think it's daytime and you will find it harder to sleep. Teenagers need more sleep than adults, as you know from when I explained about teenage brain differences in **Is Stress Different for Teenagers?**

Second, the devices are usually what will bring arguments or stresses into your life just when you need to relax. Again, that stress will make it much more difficult to sleep.

Third, the noise, bright lights and the invisible waves emitted by these gadgets can raise your heart rate and, again, make it harder to sleep. So, your parents are right...

To be honest, everyone should do this. We are all likely to sleep better if the hour before bed and then the hours during the night are an electronic-free time.

"Sometimes my evening is wrecked by arguments with friends and people from school."

It's very hard to switch off a phone or whatever device the argument is happening on, but switching it off is the best thing. Otherwise you will be tempted to react instantly and instant reactions of anger are almost always a bad idea. It's much better to wait till the next day, but waiting is hard, and the temptation is often too much if the phone is right there. So, switch it off before anything happens, and do something else. Then tell yourself how much less stressful your evening was and remember that feeling for the next day.

> "My parents have banned me from some social networks/have taken away my computer or phone because bad stuff kept happening to me.
> So now I don't tell them stuff. Why did they punish me when it wasn't my fault?"

Good question and it's something I hadn't thought of until recently, to be honest. But you're right: if your parents ban you from the internet or take away your phone because of something bad that happened to you, they are punishing the wrong person. But they probably haven't thought of this because they want to protect you. Since your parents must care about you to do that, why not explain to them that you're being punished when you're not the person who did wrong?

However, when you're in the middle of an argument or someone's said something nasty to you, your parents are doing the caring and sensible thing to take the phone away till everything calms down. Why, if it's not your fault? Because you'd be tempted to respond and it's better for you if you don't.

In the old days, when we were angry we would write a

letter. Then we'd leave the letter until the morning before going to post it; in the morning, we'd often decide not to post it. But now it's too easy for people of any age to respond in anger, instantly, before engaging the sensible parts of the brain. If you think things through, you could come up with a much better way to deal with the problem.

> "I said some stupid things online when I was thirteen and now I'm embarrassed and I want to get rid of them."

Older teenagers or people in their twenties often realize that what they said when they were younger was stupid and embarrassing. And so are some of the photos they posted. Younger people can be forgiven for saying silly things or acting thoughtlessly. But there are stories of employers checking up on this stuff later. To be honest, I think you should forgive yourself for what you said when you were younger and try to move on. When you're applying for jobs later, yes, employers may look at how you are behaving, but I don't believe they will take any notice of what you said or did when you were thirteen. What's important is what you do from now on.

SUGGESTED STRATEGIES
AND THINGS TO THINK ABOUT:

● Make a new start. From now on, only say online

the things you'd say in public. Imagine that anyone might hear. Think about what kind of public picture you want to paint of yourself. Stick to it.

● You can create a new email address and a new persona for social media. You can delete your existing accounts, if you wish.

● Forgive yourself for what you said in the past. If necessary, apologise to anyone you hurt. Then move on.

● If you know and trust an adult who is knowledgeable about online behaviour and the technical side, ask their advice about removing the stuff you don't like, or making it harder to find.

● You can often delete comments and photos you've put online (though not always). Sometimes, depending on the circumstances, you can get the website owner to take down your contributions or account. If you ask them, they should do this. They're your words and you own the rights to what happens to them.

● Do try to think about what you say. I know it's hard to look ahead to the time when you'll be job-hunting, but surveys suggest that almost half of employers make some judgements about a candidate's personality based on Facebook profiles. And when something becomes more popular than Facebook, you can be pretty sure employers will look at that, too. There are also free programs that can analyse your tweets or the things that you "Like" on Facebook, and claim to assess your personality and even intelligence through them. Very scary, if you ask me. As I said, they probably won't worry *too* much about what you said aged thirteen, but you never know. And it has happened.

If you can get through your whole adolescence without making a mistake or having a problem with social media, then you are amazing and amazingly lucky. Most people will make mistakes. What we need to do is learn from them and move on.

"There're some lies and horrible stuff about me online and I don't know what to do about it."

"What can I do about an embarrassing picture that's online?"

There is an organisation called CEOP, which stands for Child Exploitation and Online Protection. They will help you, find someone for you to talk to and show you how to get the bad stuff taken down. See the resources section of this book for their website and a link to videos on how to report images and get them taken down.

It is against the law to publish or pass around indecent videos or pictures of anyone under the age of eighteen. This law will help you get the material taken down.

Finding bad stuff about you online – whether untrue or nasty or plain embarrassing – is an incredibly stressful feeling. You need help to deal with it, not just practical help but emotional help. In time, everything will fade and become part of the past and you will learn some valuable lessons from it, even if you didn't do anything wrong in the first place. Sometimes we have to find out the hard way.

Exams and Schoolwork

"Exams, whilst important, aren't the be all and end all of life, the universe and everything."
Malorie Blackman, author

"My biggest stress is failing exams at the end of the year." **Michael, 16**

"Plans change – it doesn't matter whether you know exactly what your plans are after school or not, once you get out there things happen and the plans go out of the window. And that's not necessarily a bad thing." **Rebecca, adult**

"Don't be afraid to ask for help, it doesn't make you stupid, it confirms how wise you really are for questioning information you are given."
Sarah, adult

"When you know you've studied and worked hard enough for your exam, and then you see the paper and you're like, 'What even is this?' then it becomes stressful."
Rebecca, 16

"My two older brothers are both geniuses. My parents expect me to get the same amazing grades but I'm just not that smart. I feel like I'll disappoint them if I don't do well in my exams."
Jessica, 16

When I was researching for this book, I did several informal surveys to find out what teenagers worried about most. The notable result was that one thing worries teenagers of all ages far, far more than anything else: exams.

Teenagers in the UK face more exams than when I was at school in the 1970s. In my day, you had public exams twice, once in the final term and once two years before. No continuous assessment, just a very nasty few weeks of exams during those two summers. So, in terms of stress,

172

our bodies geared up with huge "fight or flight" chemicals, but then calmed down again. That's what bodies are designed for.

But you have three, sometimes four, whole years of constant pressure. I know you can retake modules, which we couldn't do, but the pressure never lets up. So, it's not surprising you're stressed. Also, parents seem to worry more now than my parents' generation did. There's more competition, more publicity and pressure in the media, and more emphasis on going to university, regardless of whether it's right for you.

The trick is to manage the pressure so you can deal with it and achieve your best in the exams. This isn't a book about how to revise for exams or about exam technique, so I'm going to focus on making the stress manageable.

There are some strategies that apply to all types of exam stress. I'll give you those first and then I'll mention some specific worries some of you have and give you separate advice for those.

SUGGESTED STRATEGIES
FOR EVERYONE LEADING UP TO EXAMS:

O Find out how you work best and control your environment. Some people work better on their own, others in groups; some with music, others with silence; some at the kitchen table, others in their own room; some at a desk, some on the floor; some in a tidy room, others in a messy room.

- Ask your adults to help you create that environment. For example, if you have brothers or sisters who are getting in the way, and you need peace and quiet, make sure the adults know what you need and help you achieve it.

- However, don't expect younger brothers or sisters to understand. They can't. You may need to get away by going to work somewhere else, such as a library or café.

- Discover and use your own learning styles: some people learn better when they write things down, others respond to reading the work aloud. If mind-mapping works for you, use that, but don't fret if it doesn't – everyone is different.

- But learning styles can change over time, so don't get stuck in an "I can only learn when I'm writing notes" rut. Be open to other methods that might also work.

- Ask for help early.

- Create a revision timetable and make sure it's realistic and includes time for relaxation.

- Eat well. Snack on good brain foods before you work and before an exam. Some food suggestions follow later.

- Get the best sleep you can. Advice follows later.

- Make sure you know exactly how each exam works, for example, how many questions you'll need to answer.
- If you haven't done exams before, talk to people who have, so they can give you tips. But remember that everyone is different.
- Be as prepared as you can be as early as you can be. Be like an athlete getting ready for a big competition – preparation is the key.
- Be kind to yourself.

High-achievers

"What if I don't get the grades I need?"

"My teachers and parents expect me to do well but I'm so worried I won't."

"I can't tell my friends how stressed I am about exams because they just say I have nothing to worry about because I'm clever – they don't understand."

"I desperately want to be really successful and get a good job but what if I don't?"

No one can tell you what results you will get or whether you will be lucky on the day. And it's good to aim high, to be ambitious, to risk failure. The fact that you are aiming so high gives you a very, very good chance of succeeding in life – but that may not mean now, with these exams. It's not the end of the world if you don't get the grades you think you need. Yes, you'll be disappointed, maybe bitterly disappointed, but the world won't stop. You can then pick yourself up, show true strength of character and find another way to achieve your dreams. There are always other ways, whether it's taking the exams again later, choosing another college, taking some time to grow your brain.

Almost every really successful person has had to deal with failure, cope with not achieving what they wanted at the start. I had twenty-one years of being rejected before I had my first novel published. Every rejection was a bitter blow and sometimes I nearly gave up, but I wanted it enough that I picked myself up and tried to do better next time. Anyone who survives setbacks comes back stronger. And failing an exam is only a setback. It is not the end of your dreams.

SUGGESTED STRATEGIES
AND THINGS TO THINK ABOUT:

- Be positive; aim to do your best but tell yourself that you *will* cope if it goes wrong. Because you will.
- Make sure your parents aren't expecting too

much; tell them you're really worried and that it stresses you that they assume you'll do well.

- Be careful to look after your health while you're under pressure.
- Don't give up all your hobbies. Hobbies and exercise can help your brain unwind and make you able to retain new information better.
- Failing exams is not failure; it's a challenge.
- Exams are not the most important thing in the world and are not the only route to success.

People who find schoolwork hard

"I think I'm doing the wrong subjects."

"There's way too much to do."

"Everyone else seems more organised/ less worried than me."

"I missed some work and I can't catch up."

"I'm really trying but I just can't do it. I just sit in front of my books and nothing goes in."

"I can't be bothered – I don't see the point of any of it."

All these thoughts and problems are very common. It's a

kind of minor panic state and it's very unpleasant. People of all levels of "intelligence" have these worries sometimes.

SUGGESTED STRATEGIES
AND THINGS TO THINK ABOUT:

- Talk to your teachers in the subjects you are worried about. Don't wait till the problem gets worse.
- If you've missed any work through illness or just because you didn't understand, your teacher can (and must) help you catch up. The teacher might have forgotten. Ask now – don't wait.
- If you think your friends are more organised than you, ask them to help you.
- If you need help with organisation – especially if you have dyslexia or dyspraxia – ask for it. Teachers are trained to help and if one teacher can't help you, ask another.
- If you are sitting in front of your books and nothing's going in, I know the feeling! Just reading something doesn't work for lots of people. So, try to do something with the information. Write it down and read it aloud. Make rhymes and pictures for it. You can also try putting it into your own words, or explaining it to a friend, anything apart from just reading it.
- Perhaps you need to drop a subject. Why not discuss this with the teacher?

Panic in exams

"I sometimes panic in exams."

"I had a panic attack once and I'm terrified of it happening again."

"My mind sometimes goes blank in exams."

"I'm just one of those people who can't remember things under pressure."

Again, these are common problems. Most adults will have experienced them in the past, but you may need to remind them.

SUGGESTED STRATEGIES AND THINGS TO THINK ABOUT:

- You need good relaxation techniques, strategies that you can use very quickly in an exam, with no one looking. You'll find relaxation and anti-panic strategies in *SECTION THREE*. Practise them during the weeks before the exam so you know what to do when the time comes.

- Just because you had a panic attack once doesn't mean you'll have one again. In fact, because you know what to look out for, you should be able to stop it happening when you spot the signs.

179

- Never spend time worrying over one question. Find a question you can do and then come back to the other ones later. Sounds obvious? Not to everyone. If you have OCD, you may feel you have to do the questions in order. You don't.
- Do you like fiddling or doodling? Take a stress ball into the exam. It really helps some people. Or doodle on a spare piece of paper.

A tragic problem

Every year, there are always a few terrible stories of young people, often incredibly talented ones, taking their own lives because they found the pressure of exams too much. This is shocking, tragic, and so unnecessary. If you ever feel a sense of despair, or that a huge black cloud is wrapping you up and stopping you from breathing and seeing, or if you are worried that a friend is getting things out of proportion, please, please, please, get help. Tell someone. Exams can warp your mind so much that you think there's no way out, that things will never get better. But everyone else who has been through them will tell you: exams just don't matter that much. Life is a million times more important, and your life can be wonderful whatever happens in exams.

A final and important point

I want to repeat this: exams don't matter as much as you

might think. Teachers and parents obviously want you to do your best, and schools spend enormous effort focusing on these measurements of success. But in their effort to push you to achieve your best, they sometimes make it seem as though if you don't do well in exams your life will be a failure. Certainly, getting good results is one step towards some types of success, but it is not the only measure of ability and it is not the only way to succeed.

I know many, many people who didn't get the grades they wanted at school, or who went to pieces or were ill during exams, or wanted to go to university but couldn't, or who did go to university but dropped out, and they all now have successful careers and lives. Many young people are pushed towards a particular job or course because they can't think of anything else, but there are plenty of other possibilities that you don't know about when you are at school.

So, do the very best you can to give yourself the most options and the easiest journey later, but never get into a state of mind where you think that these exams are your only chance of a successful and happy life. They are not.

Other schoolwork stress

"I can't decide what subjects to take.
I want to be with my friends but they don't
like the same things as me."

181

"I can't decide whether to do things I like
or things that will be useful to me."

"I keep changing my mind – it's a nightmare!"

It sometimes feels as though too much is going on at
school and that you are making huge decisions that are
going to affect your whole life if you get them wrong.

*"This is the point when we are meant to start
studying but with the amount of homework
and clubs the school pushes us to complete and
attend, how are we meant to find time to study?"*
Laura, 16

———

*"We seem to have our whole life ahead of us and
there's so much that we're too young to do, yet we're
expected to make all these, like, decisions that could
potentially ruin us when we're grown up and I don't
feel I'm ready for all this responsibility."*
Amy, 16

———

*"The pressure from school to social life is
overwhelming. There just never seem to be enough
hours in the day to cram it all in."*
Alyse, 16

———

"At my age a whole new selection of commitments come into play. For example we have to choose subjects. This may seem easy but causes a lot of stress. There are many factors that make it stressful, such as only picking the subjects you are good at and not the ones you enjoy. Another is picking subjects with your friends. If you don't pick subjects that your friends pick then chances are you won't see them as much and that could cause you to drift apart. Picking subjects as you can see has lots of factors that cause people to stress. (Big time!)"

Kirsty, 13

SUGGESTED STRATEGIES
AND THINGS TO THINK ABOUT:

● There must be a teacher who can help you decide whether you should do the subjects you like or whether you'd be wise to pick more strategically. (It does depend on your individual strengths, so I can't generalise, but most people would agree that you shouldn't do subjects you don't actually like.)

● I wouldn't recommend choosing simply to be with your friends, because you're bound to make other friends in your new subjects. You don't have to lose touch with old friends, anyway.

● If you later find you've made the wrong choice, you can almost always change. We're allowed to make wrong decisions; in fact, we learn from them. What counts is what you do when you realize it's happened. Generally speaking, the advice is: don't panic; talk to someone who knows (eg, for school subjects, a teacher); get help in putting the decision right. There is almost always a way.

● It's usually better to choose subjects you enjoy, if possible, partly because you are going to have to spend a lot of time on them and partly because enjoying a subject does make it easier to do well in it. Also, most jobs and careers have lots of different pathways to them, and it's almost always possible to add in some new skills or courses to fill any gaps.

"I've got dyslexia and it's becoming
so much more of a problem now because
we have to write so much."

"I struggle to Keep up with everyone – I just
think I'm thick."

"My parents want me to go to university
but I really don't want to."

"I have a really bad relationship with the teacher of the subject I really need to do."

Those are very different worries but I've put them together because they all have one answer: talk about this to a trusted adult because there is help for you, whatever the school-related problem. (For dyslexia and other learning difficulties, see **Specific learning difficulties**.)

You may think it's hard to take your worries to a teacher but they don't want you to be struggling and suffering alone. And the sooner you get help, the easier it will be to solve the problem.

"I just can't cope with all the homework."

"The thing that stresses me out is homework."
Sean, 16

———

"Teachers tell you to start studying yet they pile a lot of homework on you at the same time."
Emma, 16

———

"The biggest stress is trying to get all your homework completed on time whilst trying to find time to study." **Claire, 16**

———

"The thing that stresses me out at the moment is my homework. I never seem to have enough time to do it." **Michael, 16**

———————

This is a really common stress but there are quite simple ways to deal with it.

SUGGESTED STRATEGIES AND THINGS TO THINK ABOUT:

- Talk to your parents or carers – they may have practical suggestions, such as creating a manageable schedule and making a good space for you to work.
- Talk to your teachers – if they know you're struggling, they will try to help.
- Team up with a friend and work collaboratively.
- Make lists and plans – a written schedule often helps clarify things.
- You need breaks – you'll work better after a quick walk.

"Success is a deeply personal matter. For some people success means fame, or wealth, or possessions, or popularity, or qualifications, or trophies. But for me success is something far

simpler: it's about knowing that you've done your best, irrespective of what other people think of you. This may not be the kind of success you'll read about in celebrity magazines, but it's success that you can see all around you. People who work hard, face difficulties with courage, act with kindness and generosity, help others, pick themselves up when things go wrong, do their best at all times – these to me are the most successful people, and if I can stand alongside them, I'm more than happy."

Tim Bowler, author

Sleep

Sleep is a major problem for many teenagers. Adults often joke about how dopey teenagers are in the mornings but sleep loss is no joking matter.

There are three main ways in which sleep problems and stress go together: first, stress very often makes it harder to get a good night's sleep. Second, not being able to get to sleep or stay asleep is stressful in itself, as you worry about feeling terrible in the morning. Third, poor sleep over a number of nights or weeks or months affects your schoolwork, because it is harder to concentrate and remember things when you are sleep deprived; and if your schoolwork is affected, you'll be even more anxious. When I ask teenagers which stress symptoms they often suffer from, "Lying awake worrying about something" is easily the most common answer.

SECTION TWO

> *"Everyone wants a piece of me right now.*
> *School overload, trying to balance a social life while*
> *also trying to get to sleep at night when my head is in*
> *a blended mode of: eatsleepstudyfriendsfamilychill."*
> **Eilidh, 16**

Let me start with the problem of not being able to get to sleep at the beginning of the night, as this is different from some other sleep problems which involve waking during the night.

"After I switch my light out I take ages – hours sometimes – to get to sleep."

"My brain seems to race. I'm tired but my thoughts just won't switch off."

The causes and solutions are different for different people but it's likely that at least one of the following suggestions will be relevant to you. And I certainly recommend that you try all the strategies in **Get a good night's sleep** in *SECTION THREE*. Our brains easily fall into patterns or habits. Breaking a bad habit takes a bit of patience but you will be surprised how a few days of trying new strategies make a huge difference. Our brains learn fast.

SUGGESTED STRATEGIES
AND THINGS TO THINK ABOUT:

- The teenage brain has different sleep patterns from other ages. Your body clock partly follows adult patterns, making you sleepy from around 11 p.m. If you try to sleep before you are sleepy, there's a good chance you won't be able to. Then you'll worry that you can't sleep and the worry will make it even harder to sleep. You might think a solution is to go to bed later but the problem with that is teenagers actually need more sleep than adults (9.25 hours on average). So, *somehow* you need to feel sleepy earlier. My next suggestions are about this.

- The body clock responds to daylight. So, to make your brain think it's late, you need to make it think it's dark. Close your bedroom curtains more than an hour before you start getting ready for bed, dim the lights and switch off all screens – TV, computer, tablet and phone.

189

Switch. Off. Your. Phone. (I explain why below.) Your brain won't respond immediately but if you do this for a few days, at the same time each night, your brain will notice.

- Some other things make you more awake if you do them in the evening, because they raise your heart rate. Here's a list of things to avoid for the one to two hours before you want to feel sleepy: loud or fast music; caffeine (coffee, tea and caffeinated/energy drinks); a large meal; strenuous exercise. (Gentle stretching or something like yoga is a good idea, as it's relaxing.)

- Practise the deep-breathing relaxation techniques in *SECTION THREE*.

- Use the **Get a good night's sleep** techniques in *SECTION THREE*.

- Reading a book or magazine before you sleep is a good idea. It quietens the brain and helps take your mind off whatever's worrying you.

- Listening to quiet, relaxing, slow music is helpful for the same reasons as reading.

- If you are troubled by thoughts spinning round your brain, practise the **Controlling your thoughts** techniques in *SECTION THREE*.

- Make yourself think of something happy – or boring. Happy things could be daydreams and imagined stories in which your fantasy comes true – whether it's being a hero or having some amazing kind of success. See **Deliberate daydreaming** in *SECTION THREE*. Boring things could be reliving journeys that you know well – for example, picture yourself walking to the shops, thinking of each bit in as much detail as you possibly can. This is very similar to the old trick of counting sheep, just slightly less boring. The basic reason is the same: to stop you thinking of the things that are keeping you awake, and to lull you into sleepiness.

○ Don't *think* about trying to go to sleep. The more you think about it, or being tired in the morning, the less likely you are to sleep. Just remind yourself that actually a few bad nights' sleep are not going to make any difference.

○ Use the time to plan something that needs to be planned – a friend's birthday, for example. I use these times to plan whatever story I want to write next. It's amazing (and worrying) how quickly that sends me to sleep...

"When I'm lying awake during the night, all my worries seem huge. I can't stop thinking about them."

"I get to sleep fine but I always wake in the

191

middle of the night/really early in the morning
and can't get back to sleep."

"I look at my clock and Keep seeing how little time
I've got left to sleep and I panic because I Know I'll
feel horrible in the morning."

I reckon everyone reading this knows the feeling of lying awake and thinking that everyone else is sleeping soundly. All your worries crowd in on you; negative thoughts spiral; even things you don't worry about during the day suddenly seem huge. It's as though there's a special bit of your brain that comes to life as soon as you want to go to sleep and all your worries are suddenly free to dance and shout. There is no such part of the brain...

SUGGESTED STRATEGIES
AND THINGS TO THINK ABOUT:

- All the last four points from the previous set of strategies apply equally to the night-time waking problem.
- Waking very early and not being able to get back to sleep is sometimes linked to depression. If you also feel very sad during the day and have a sense of pointlessness about your life, I recommend you talk to your GP. People with depression often think no one can help them – in fact, that's a common symptom – please

believe me when I say that there are people out there who can.

"What should I do when I can't get to sleep - Keep trying or give up?"

There's some disagreement about this. Some people think that it's best just to lie there, thinking peaceful thoughts and practising some of the strategies I've already mentioned. Other people say you shouldn't lie awake too long in bed.

SUGGESTED STRATEGIES AND THINGS TO THINK ABOUT:

- If you've been lying wide awake for more than twenty minutes, switching on a small light and reading (not a screen) for a few minutes can help. It does depend what time it is, too. If it's five o'clock in the morning, it might be worth getting up and using the time to do something useful since you're awake. But if it's one o'clock in the morning it would be better to stay in bed and either read for a while or practise relaxation techniques.

- The main thing is stop thinking about *trying* to go to sleep. It almost never works. Sleep comes when we're not trying. So, what you do

193

depends on whether you're lying there getting very stressed and being battered by negative thoughts or feeling quite peaceful.

● If you can't get rid of negative thoughts, putting the light on and reading is a good idea because it will distract you from those thoughts. Just don't go on the internet or switch your phone on...

● The other thing you shouldn't do is panic. Don't lie there thinking how awful you're going to feel in the morning. You won't! A few nights of bad sleep are perfectly manageable and people cope on much less sleep than they'd like.

Sleeping medicines

Never take any sleeping pills without a doctor's prescription. Sleeping pills have major risks, mainly of addiction and dependence. Some herbal remedies are OK but always check with a pharmacist or doctor before taking them. Even with herbal remedies there's a risk that you will believe that you can't go to sleep without them, so they should only be used carefully and for short periods of time when you especially need to sleep.

Look out for products (such as herbal teas) with these ingredients: passiflora, lavender, hops, camomile and valerian. But note: just because a remedy is "herbal" does not mean it is weak. Valerian and passiflora are examples of herbs that must be taken according to the recommended dose. The safe way is to buy them as herbal teas – not pills etc – and just drink one mug before bed. One side-effect of taking too strong herbal sleep remedies is feeling groggy in the morning and you don't want this.

Alcohol and sleep

Alcohol doesn't help anyone get a good night's sleep. It makes people sleepy (when they've had a lot) but it makes them wake in the middle of the night, too. It disrupts healthy sleep patterns. Also, drinking so much that you fall asleep harms your brain. It destroys brain cells and you can't repair them. Alcohol is also highly addictive.

The problem with electronic screens and phones

Remember I said that turning off screens and phones was important for falling asleep more easily? Here's why:

- Backlit screens mimic daylight, even if they don't seem very bright. It is the same sort of light – it looks white, though it's actually called blue light. The devices you hold within a metre of your face – such as computers, tablets and phones – are likely to bring that daylight close enough to your eyes to trick your brain into thinking it's daytime. (In fact, scientists say that all lights, even normal light bulbs, encourage our brains to think it's daytime, but blue light has a stronger effect.)

- Engaging with these screens involves potentially "wakening" things – exciting films, loud music, flickering lights, competitive games, lots of information. These all keep your brain awake, and make it feel jangly for some time afterwards.

- Being on social media and receiving phone calls or texts are likely to make you stressed at just the time when you need to switch off. Even expecting or worrying about or wanting a message to come is likely to make you unrelaxed. The only way to prevent this is to have the gadgets entirely switched off – and, ideally, not in your room at all during the night.

- When these gadgets are switched on (even if you aren't using them) they produce electromagnetic radiation. There's now quite a lot of research suggesting that this has a negative effect on sleep. It may also have other negative effects such as preventing your body from repairing itself as well as it is supposed to during sleep. This is especially a problem with mobile phones, partly because they are likely to be closest to you. So, don't sleep with them in your room, or turn them off (not just onto silent).

Alcohol and Drugs

Many teenagers take dangerous risks with alcohol and drugs. Taking some risks in life is important but the part of the brain that lets us make good choices about this is the prefrontal cortex – which doesn't fully develop until well into your twenties. The good news is that increasing numbers of young people now do choose to avoid alcohol and drugs – join them!

When teenagers use alcohol, they do it for many reasons: because taking risks can be fun, because of peer pressure or the desire for rebellion, and because it can make you feel more confident and relaxed. Also, although most teenagers know they shouldn't do it, they may not understand or believe the danger.

The motivations for using drugs are similar. The dangers are sometimes different, because the laws are different and because we know less about the effects of some drugs. In this book, when I say "alcohol" I'm usually also including drugs.

The truth is that both alcohol and drugs are extremely dangerous for a whole load of reasons. And you may not know that they affect teenagers more than adults, for reasons that we don't exactly understand, except that the teenage brain just seems to be extra vulnerable.

You risk:

◉ Breaking the law and getting a criminal record. This

can affect your job chances and freedom to travel, for example. Although drinking alcohol itself is not against the law, it often leads to committing a crime, with the majority of youth crime being alcohol-related. Using other drugs is a crime, with varying penalties. (So-called "legal highs" keep being reclassified, so it's often hard to know what is or isn't against the law.) Passing drugs to or for someone else, even if you aren't selling them, is a serious offence. Never handle drugs for anyone else, for any reason whatsoever. Lives have been ruined like this.

- Having an accident or causing an accident.
- Having sex when you didn't want to. (Because when you are drunk you do things you wouldn't otherwise do.)
- Becoming seriously ill (or dying) from alcohol-related problems.
- Dying from a single use of certain drugs – allergic reactions to drugs such as Ecstasy have been known to cause death. You or your friends may think they know how to be safe, but the truth is that no one, not even an adult, knows how to stay safe with some drugs.
- Becoming addicted. (If you start drinking alcohol or taking drugs before the age of 15, you are at far greater risk of addiction later.)

● Destroying brain cells (which doctors currently cannot repair for you). Brain cells and connections are destroyed by being drunk and almost certainly by drug abuse, too. This damage seems to happen more and in more important areas in teenagers.

In short, you risk ruining your life. Sorry to be so tough about this but I feel very strongly about it because I know what alcohol does. It's best to know the risks in advance so that you can avoid the dangers and help your friends avoid them, too.

Of course, most people don't die or have a terrible accident, or suffer noticeable long-term damage. So, you might decide to take the risk. Like flipping a coin with your life. Thing is, your brain is the only one you've got and its health makes such a difference to your success and happiness. I just don't think it's a risk worth taking.

These warnings might have made you more stressed, and this book is supposed to help you be less stressed. But don't worry, because whatever damage has happened already to your brain, you're young and it is not too late to decide to stop the damage and start to look after it. If you can make the most of your brain from now on, that's the best way to carry you through life.

Let's look at some of the worries you may have.

"I've been drinking quite a lot.

Have I really damaged my brain?"

"I got really drunk at a party. I didn't mean to - I couldn't tell what I was drinking."

OK, so when you get drunk you lose brain connections which you may not be able to repair. And we don't know how many cells or exactly which ones they will be. The points below will reassure you, if you look after your brain from now on.

SUGGESTED STRATEGIES
AND THINGS TO THINK ABOUT:

● You have a lot of spare brain cells and connections. You would have to get drunk often – but no one knows how often – before the damage would be a problem. This sounds vague because the truth is vague: we just don't know how many brain cells we can afford to damage, but the chances are very good that you will not notice any loss of ability because of getting drunk a few times.

● Although we can't repair our brain cells, the brain is often quite good at working round a loss by creating new connections between other cells. So, if we damage some cells and connections, we can avoid losing skills by working hard to create new brain connections. It depends on where you've lost connections, how good your brain was in the first place, and how often you practise the skills you need to reinforce. Basically, if you lose too many cells in certain places, it becomes harder to learn and remember and think – not impossible, just harder. If you try hard, you'll improve hugely, because that's how the brain works. So, stop further damage by not getting drunk again, and keep exercising your brain by practising the skills you want to keep.

● Although the teenage brain is vulnerable, all the natural changes that are happening also give it the possibility of great development. So, don't worry too much about what you've done in the past. Your job now is to improve your future. You can do this simply by trying, which is how the brain learns and develops and becomes strong.

"My friends all get drunk/take drugs sometimes and I feel I have to go along with them otherwise I look like a wimp."

"When I go to a party I don't really want to get drunk because I don't like it much, but stuff always gets out of control and I go along with it because everyone else is."

Always tricky. This dilemma is something most adults can relate to. It's hard not to go along with your friends and we know the power of peer pressure and the importance of fitting in. The trouble is that it's not always the guilty ones who get caught; so, you're risking getting into trouble for something you didn't even want to do. It's a shame to put your body and brain at risk for something you're not even enjoying.

SUGGESTED STRATEGIES AND THINGS TO THINK ABOUT:

- You're not the only teenager who doesn't want to drink or take drugs. All the statistics show that in fact most teenagers don't regularly get drunk (though many will have an accidental or occasional bad encounter with alcohol) or take drugs. If you want to avoid it, you are actually in the majority. It's just that you are the quiet majority. So, if you know other friends who don't want to get involved, stick with them.

- If your friends are doing something that you don't want to do, are they, in the long-term, going to be your friends? It seems to me that you're probably going to drift away from them sooner or later anyway. Is it perhaps time to look for some new friends?

- Try to get involved in activities where drinking or

drugs aren't part of the scene. Sport, for example: most athletes avoid those substances because it weakens their fitness. Usually, when people are busy and enjoying an activity, they don't need alcohol or drugs which are often used to deal with boredom.

"There's a party coming up and I know there's going to be alcohol. I don't want to miss the fun but I'm worried about what's going to happen."

"My friend's parents are going away and she's having a house party without them knowing. I'm worried that something bad will happen."

You have a tough decision ahead. If you are worried that the drinking will get out of hand the sensible decision is not to go. But how?

SUGGESTED STRATEGIES AND THINGS TO THINK ABOUT:

- You could say you're not feeling well on the day. That way you won't upset anyone or make anyone think you're being silly.
- You could say your parents won't let you.
- If this party is happening without the host's

parents knowing, then there is an extra risk. The best (but very difficult) thing is not to go if you're at all worried. If something goes wrong, you will become tangled up in the fallout and, being a decent person, you'll feel guilty...

● One option is to go to the party but leave at the first sign of trouble. To keep control, you will need to avoid alcohol, but you can always pretend to drink if necessary. You'll also need to plan how to get home safely – for example, to arrange in advance for someone to pick you up or have the number and money for a trusted taxi firm. Plan ahead: money, phone (with battery charged), any numbers you need, and make sure there's an adult at home if you need to come back.

"I'm worried about my friend because
I know she's drinking a lot."

"I'm worried about a friend who doesn't
seem to realize the dangers."

"I'm worried about my friend because
I know he takes drugs and hangs out with
other people who do drugs."

It's very difficult to help friends who are doing dangerous

things and you may not be able to do anything about it. If that's the case, you should not feel guilty. Of course you care, because you're a good friend, but you aren't in charge of what your friends do. But, you'll want to try, so here's some advice.

SUGGESTED STRATEGIES
AND THINGS TO THINK ABOUT:

- Think about the best way to talk to your friend. Be prepared to stay very calm if they get cross with you. The anger is most likely to be partly embarrassment.

- Don't be judgemental. Just show that you are really worried. Tell your friend that you care about their health.

- See if you can find other things to do with your friend so that they don't have the need or opportunity to drink.

- If a drug is involved, find out about it, for example from the Talk to Frank website. That website also has advice about how to help a friend.

- Can you find a way to ask your school to raise awareness of the dangers of alcohol and drugs? Many schools think they've delivered this information but it just hasn't got through. Knowing the dangers doesn't stop everyone taking the risks, but it has an effect on some people and if it stops even one or two of your friends damaging themselves, it'll be worth it. If you don't want anyone to know it was your idea, find a way of approaching a teacher privately or even anonymously.

● If you are seriously worried, perhaps because your friend's behaviour has gone way beyond occasional binge-drinking or drug-taking, get advice from an adult, such as your guidance teacher or year head. You can do this without naming your friend.

"My mum/dad/carer is often drunk and I don't know how to help."

"I'm scared about the amount of drinking my mum/dad/carer does."

I'm so sorry about this. It's a horrible thing to experience. But there are solutions and people who can help you.

SUGGESTED STRATEGIES AND THINGS TO THINK ABOUT:

● This is not something you can or should deal with by yourself. You need expert help. Start by asking any teacher you trust. They can't cure the problem but they will know who can help you.

If you have a social worker, talk to them. You can talk confidentially to your GP, too.

- If you can tell your parent how worried and upset you are, then do. Show them how desperately you want them to get help and reassure them that you will also help but explain that you can't do it on your own because you don't know enough. Usually, an alcoholic just doesn't see the effect they're having on the family and they may deny it because it's too painful; but sometimes your response could be enough to push them to get help.

- If you ever feel physically in danger – or if you think they are in danger – get help immediately. If you have to dial 999, then do. You could be saving yourself and your parent.

- Alcoholism is a massive and frightening problem. You cannot and should not deal with it on your own. There are resources at the end of this book. If you can't decide which to use, phone Childline.

"My dad is an alcoholic and so was his mother – I'm worried that I might inherit it."

People worry about all sorts of things they might have inherited from their parents, including personality. I want you to stop worrying about this right now.

SUGGESTED STRATEGIES
AND THINGS TO THINK ABOUT:

- It's true that the tendency towards addiction can be partly genetic. But even if you have inherited the genes, you do *not* have to be affected by them. In fact, because you are more aware of it and worried about it, you could even be less likely than other people to become addicted. Being extra alert to the risks can give you the strength to say no.

- If you drink at the age of 15 or under, you have a slightly higher chance of becoming an alcoholic – a good extra reason for being really careful to avoid it or to stop if you have already started. When someone asks why you don't drink, you can say that you've seen what alcohol does to people and you don't want to go down that route.

"I want to know the truth about drugs and alcohol but everyone says different things."

The resources at the end of this book are the most trustworthy I can find. Talk to Frank is an especially clear site with lots of advice on individual drugs and ways to get help for you or a friend.

Here are the main points about drugs:

- Drugs alter your brain. Some of these effects are temporary and some are longer-term or permanent. Experts don't fully understand the long-term results of all drugs, though they're learning more about some of them.

- Cannabis is the most commonly used drug, though it is becoming less popular. It is a Class B drug and it's illegal to possess it, even for personal use. The penalty for supplying it to someone else (even giving it free to a friend) is up to 14 years in prison.

- Cannabis usually makes you feel relaxed and calm, but it can also make you agitated and paranoid. If you use it regularly, it is linked to mental illness, such as depression and even schizophrenia.

- If someone offers you a pill or powder, you have no way of knowing what it really is. Therefore, the risks are huge.

- Some drugs react dangerously with alcohol.

Here are the main points about alcohol:

- It is safest not to drink alcohol before the age of fifteen.

- Alcohol is a depressant. Yes, at first it makes you excited and happy, but it soon depresses mood and reactions. It makes some people very aggressive and everyone more likely to take bad risks.

- People are different but on average it takes about an hour for the body to get rid of one unit of alcohol. (See below for an explanation of units of alcohol.)
- The problem with spirits, particularly vodka, is that you usually don't know how much is in your glass. Sweet, fruity drinks disguise the bitter taste of alcohol and you're likely to drink more than you think.
- It takes about half an hour to feel the full effects of alcohol, so if you drink too quickly you may not realize you're getting drunk until too late.
- Binge-drinking is defined as drinking six units in one evening or day for women and eight for men; for teenagers, five units is binge-drinking. You can see from these amounts that you could be binge-drinking after a small number of drinks. That is risking your health, your safety, your future and your life. And wrecking your brain.

HOW TO TELL HOW
MUCH ALCOHOL YOU ARE DRINKING

"One unit of alcohol" is not the same as "one drink" because different drinks have different amounts of alcohol in them. You can work out the amount of alcohol in any drink by looking at the % sign on the bottle/can. If it says 12%, it means there would be 12 units of alcohol in a whole litre of that drink. Some bottles will tell you how many units in that bottle, which is easy to understand. Some bottles will say how many units in each portion or measurement of that drink, but the problem is you might not know how much they mean by a portion.

Some examples:

- One large (250ml) glass of normal 12% wine would contain around 3 units of alcohol
- Half a pint of 3.5% strength beer/lager is about 1 unit
- Half a pint of premium beer/lager (5%) is 1.5 units
- A single shot of vodka is 1 unit – but sometimes there might be more than one shot in the glass you are given
- A small bottle (275ml) of strong cider is 2.3 units
- A pint of super strength beer is about 4 units

To sum up my advice on alcohol and drugs: don't worry if you've done it in the past but do stop now. Please!

Special Physical and Mental Challenges

There are certain conditions you might already have before you become a teenager, which can make adolescence harder. With some, it can be difficult to tell which stresses are caused by just being a teenager and which are made worse by your condition. And some things get worse while you are a teenager, partly because you are beginning to try to make your own decisions.

There are also things that might happen in your teenage years which have nothing to do with being a teenager – such as bereavement or your parents divorcing. And those things can affect teenagers differently from children or adults.

For all of these things, my advice begins in the same way:

- Learn about your condition. Find websites or books that focus on young people.
- Find others going through the same thing. Use responsible websites and self-help groups that your GP surgery can tell you about, or see the resources at the back of this book.
- Don't suffer alone. Talk to a trusted adult. If you can't think of someone to talk to, phone a helpline provided by the organisation that focuses on your condition, or phone Childline.

Specific learning difficulties
– dyslexia, dyspraxia, dyscalculia

Dyslexia literally means "poor reading and writing" but has many different forms and includes other symptoms. It is not always obvious, because some people with dyslexia can spell and write quite normally and may seem to read quite normally, too.

Dyspraxia often overlaps with dyslexia but is more to do with clumsiness and organisation. Dyspraxic people have huge difficulty keeping time, knowing where they are meant to be and having the right things with them.

Dyscalculia causes difficulties with numbers and maths.

All these conditions can be diagnosed in children as young as seven (with some signs earlier) or as late as adulthood.

How do these conditions affect teenagers especially?
They can seem more of a problem during your teenage years because you are expected to be more independent than when you were at primary school. Also, you have to read and write more and to organise yourself, moving between classrooms and remembering complicated time-tables. If teachers don't realize you have extra problems, or if they don't understand dyslexia etc, they may be impatient. Explain your special challenges to them, and that you need extra time for the particular things you find hard.

Exams will probably be a major challenge for you. If you have a proper diagnosis of one of these conditions, you will be allowed extra time in public exams and this can help hugely. You can only have this extra time if you have had a proper assessment, so your parents may have to push for this. If your writing is a problem, you may be allowed a "scribe", who can write down the answers you give. Make sure these strategies are in place long before the exams start, ideally at the beginning of the school year.

One piece of reassurance for girls: there's some evidence that the female hormone, oestrogen, has a positive effect on dyslexia, so you may notice an improvement without doing anything! We don't know why this happens but oestrogen seems to boost certain language skills.

For both girls and boys, your developing brain should allow you to find clever strategies to help your problems. As your brain develops, you can also understand meanings more deeply or from different angles and you should by now have a better sense of your own strengths and weaknesses and be able to work better with them. Ask for help with revision skills, as things like colours, maps, diagrams and using a voice recorder could all be useful for you. Remember that people are different in the ways they learn, so look for the methods and tips that will work for you.

SUGGESTED STRATEGIES
AND THINGS TO THINK ABOUT:

- If you think you might have any of these conditions, make sure you have the proper tests. Dyslexia is the most widely known and the initial testing can be done in school by a teacher. Then the teacher can refer you for further assessment and help if necessary. Your school probably has a learning support department, with experts in various learning difficulties.

- If your school doesn't have specially trained teachers, tell them about the Addressing Dyslexia Toolkit mentioned in the resources section. (Also tell your parents about this.)

- Although schools should usually do the initial tests, you may also need to be tested by an educational psychologist. Some schools will set this up, while others will leave it to your parents. If your parents can't find how to get the tests you need, a GP will help. Or use the dyslexia organisations in the resources section.

- You could take a free online dyslexia self-test as a starting point. The ones I found were too vague and broad to be accurate, though they do highlight some of the problems that dyslexic people have. So, they can give you a pointer, but you cannot rely on them to tell you

215

whether you definitely have dyslexia.

- Everyone has things they find more difficult than others. Dyslexia brings more challenges than, for example, not being able to sing. But it can also bring strengths, such as creative powers or an entrepreneurial spirit. Never feel that you can't do something: just recognise that you have a tougher challenge than some people but that you can excel at other things.
- School can be very tough for people with conditions such as dyslexia but you will soon be out in the wide world, where there are vast opportunities for people with your way of learning and thinking.

ADHD
(attention deficit hyperactive disorder)
and ADD
(attention deficit disorder)

ADHD and ADD make it difficult to concentrate and sit still while focusing on one task. They begin before the age of seven, so you will already know if you suffer from them, and you will probably be on a treatment. Treatment often includes medication – the best-known drug is Ritalin – but you should also have been taught strategies to help you focus and manage your behaviour. The drugs do not cure the problem, just make the symptoms better, but you don't want to be on them forever so it's important to learn to live with the problem.

How do ADHD and ADD affect teenagers especially?

Around 50% of children with ADHD will stop having symptoms before they become teenagers. But if your condition has not improved or disappeared by now, the teenage years bring extra challenges. Things like anger, stress, anxiety or sadness make it more difficult for someone who is already finding it hard to control behaviour, so you've got an extra-tough situation. Also, you are bigger and stronger, with more risk-taking possibilities available, so there are more opportunities to get into trouble. Your work is harder and your frustration may be greater.

SUGGESTED STRATEGIES
AND THINGS TO THINK ABOUT:

● The main thing to do is recognise that you have a condition which needs help, and to keep asking for that help. Schools don't always realize what's very obvious to you: that telling you to behave, or punishing you, is not the answer. They may think you're just behaving badly, so make sure they understand you're not. You're trying to do things right.

- One root of the problem is difficulty with what's called "working memory" – the very short-term memory you need in order to focus on a task. For example, if you're working out some maths, you have to remember the question, and the starting numbers, and then some more numbers, and by the time you get to putting it all together you've forgotten what you're supposed to be doing. Knowing that this is a problem means you can start to create strategies such as writing everything down as you go, saying things aloud, or making sure you've understood the first bit before moving to the next.

- Do you fidget a lot, especially when trying to concentrate? Most people with ADHD/ADD do. Teachers sometimes get annoyed when you fidget but there's evidence that it can actually help you with your work. Obviously, you mustn't disturb everyone else in class, so one solution is to have a stress ball or something else to fidget with. You can tell your teacher that scientists have even been researching into this because they believe it helps some brains to work well.

OCD (obsessive compulsive disorder)

OCD can appear during earlier childhood or adolescence or later. Some people think OCD is just about washing hands obsessively but it is much more complicated than that. When you have OCD, you have huge anxiety or fears about certain things and you have routines or "rituals" to try to prevent the things you are frightened of from happening. The rituals may look strange to other people – such as tapping things, blinking repeatedly, switching things on and off or repeatedly picking things up. You may well understand in the logical part of your brain that the anxieties and rituals don't make sense, but a deeper, stronger, more emotional part of your brain keeps making you do them "just in case".

"I used to have contamination OCD but that changed when I was 11 to intrusive thoughts and habits. That could have been my brain developing. I also had about a two year gap with barely any OCD at thirteen which could've been because I was changing, but I'm not sure. Try to find other people who have OCD to make you feel less alone. It really helps to work together to fight your OCD."
Megan, 18

219

Many people have small elements of OCD. For example, they might keep checking that they've locked the door, even though they know they have; or might not be able to send an email without checking loads of times that they haven't written an embarrassing word in it. Different people have different fears and usually they learn to deal with them and live a normal life. But OCD goes much further than this. It interferes with normal life and sufferers can spend a huge amount of time trying to avoid their fears. Often sufferers try to hide the symptoms because they know that they seem weird. And it can be utterly exhausting dealing with the thoughts rushing round your head and making you permanently anxious.

How does OCD affect teenagers especially?

Being a teenager often involves new anxieties; since OCD is based on extreme anxieties, existing symptoms may become worse. Or they may change, as the things you are frightened of change. At the same time, you are probably able to explain your fears more clearly, which is a good thing.

Another good thing about being a teenager is that you can understand yourself much better, and this gives you a new tool for dealing with OCD. But don't expect to do it on your own. As well as getting professional help, talk to people who have overcome it or who are dealing with it right now – for example, in an online forum. But make sure it's a positive and responsible one. Get an adult to help you find a group of people, whether online or in the real world, who are right for you.

If your OCD gets worse when you hit the stressful times during adolescence, make sure you have the strategies and people to help you through it. With good treatment and hard work from you, and understanding from the people around you, you can learn to have a normal attitude to fears and worries.

SUGGESTED STRATEGIES
AND THINGS TO THINK ABOUT:

- Try to be open with your family and friends about your very real fears and the reasons why you sometimes do things that may look strange to them.

- You are perhaps already seeing a doctor or counsellor but you may not have been for a while, or you may have been getting better but the symptoms have returned, or changed. So see your doctor or counsellor again, or a different one if you prefer. There may be new treatments available or another doctor might have different ideas.

- It's important to realize that although your routines and behaviours make you feel better at first, they're not the answer. It's not easy to overcome them and takes time but it is possible, and once you've done it you can live a life that isn't dominated by fears.

- The most usual treatment involves "exposure". This means deliberately letting the fear come into your mind and trying not to do your ritual for a set amount of time (say a minute or five minutes) and learning to control your stress during that time by practising breathing and relaxation skills. Search online for "Exposure and Response Prevention" to find details. A doctor might also prescribe anti-anxiety medication; it's very important only to take medicines when prescribed by a doctor, as some of them react differently with teenagers.

- Find a simple way to tell people about your condition. "I have OCD. I'm getting treatment for it but sometimes it gets on top of me." If you can joke about it, so much the better. If people tease you and make you feel uncomfortable, tell them you find it hurtful. If they don't stop, deal with it as you would bullying: tell someone.

Social Anxiety Disorder (or Social Phobia)

Almost everyone knows what it's like to feel shy or to feel

anxious when walking into a room full of people. Not knowing what to say and getting nervous before meeting people, even friends, is incredibly common. That's not Social Anxiety Disorder.

Social Anxiety Disorder, sometimes called Social Phobia, is an extreme fear of social situations, the sort of fear that makes you sweat and shake, the sort of fear that makes you *desperate* to avoid social situations.

Another aspect of the condition is that you fret excessively about what people think of you and go over and over what you've said, long after the other person will have forgotten. These anxieties are quite common for other people, too – including me! – but with a genuine sufferer this goes to extremes, preventing him or her from functioning normally.

Think of it as an extreme and disabling form of shyness and self-consciousness. It's disabling because it can prevent you from doing important things that could set you on the road to a successful and happy life.

How does Social Anxiety Disorder affect teenagers especially?

Social Anxiety Disorder isn't something you are born with and it's not something you "catch". If you were very shy and worried as a child, it probably won't have been labelled as a disorder, but it can sometimes become one when you hit the teenage years. (But most shy children *don't* develop the disorder as teenagers or adults; they either remain shy and reserved, which is quite normal, or they become less obviously shy, learning strategies to hide natural shyness.)

The teenage years are a common time for the disorder to develop, because it's a period of self-consciousness and anxiety anyway. Also, you are expected to do more things on your own and you have to make a whole new set of friends in secondary school, so that makes it hard for someone who naturally finds social situations difficult. Bullying and teasing can be a huge problem, and can make a shy or vulnerable person withdraw from situations where they may be teased – which is anywhere there are people.

SUGGESTED STRATEGIES
AND THINGS TO THINK ABOUT:

- The first thing to realize is that you are not alone. And you are not weird. Most people face challenges and this is yours.
- The second thing to realize is that it's not your fault. It can run in families so perhaps all of you could tackle it together, supporting each other.
- It's really important to try to face your fears a little bit at a time and to be proud every time you do. But you may need help. You need sympathetic adults, who understand either because

they know you well or because they have the condition themselves, or because they are trained to help. There are resources at the back of the book but also ask an adult you like and trust to help you find something that is right for your age group.

- Your doctor can also help, especially if you are getting symptoms such as panic attacks and sweating. A doctor can refer you to a specialist.

- Teenagers with an anxiety problem sometimes also suffer from eating disorders or depression and it is hugely important for you to get help and not to feel alone.

- Online forums are very helpful for people who don't thrive in social situations. They are good places to talk about your symptoms and get support. But try not to let them become the only way you socialise – use them to help you get out and about in the outside world, so that you can manage the situations that you'll need to deal with later in life.

- Always remember: there is help for every condition.

Autism and Asperger's

Since these conditions begin in very early life, you'll probably know whether you suffer from them. But some people don't get a diagnosis till later, perhaps if their parents or school didn't realize what the symptoms meant, or if the symptoms were quite mild. Asperger's is a form of autism; it's sometimes called being "on the autistic spectrum" or just "on the spectrum". But autism and Asperger's are also very different. There are many levels of autism, some involving major disability, others involving amazing skills as well as disability.

I'm going to focus on Asperger's because if you suffer from a more profound form of autism you will be getting more specialist help.

How does Asperger's affect teenagers especially?

People with Asperger's (another term is Aspies) can find positives and negatives in adolescence. The teenage years are often a time of real opportunity and self-awareness and you will probably have discovered things you excel at. There will be things you still find really hard, and you will probably still find friendships difficult, but you will be able to find strategies for dealing with social situations.

You will have more experience and understanding of other people and their behaviours. More importantly, you will have worked out the most useful ways to behave when you are with people.

Also, as a teenager, it will be easier for you to meet other people with Asperger's, either through online self-help groups or in your school. People in your year group should be more accepting of your difference – and of the differences between all of us.

People with Asperger's and some with autism often have immense learning abilities. In the resources section at the back are some books by and about high-achieving Aspies. They are fascinating people and we can all learn a lot from them. You may have a wonderful memory (like Daniel Tammet, author of *Born on a Blue Day*) or an ability to spot patterns in behaviour (like Temple Grandin, author of *Animals in Translation*). And you may have patience with detailed tasks that other people give up on. Your obsessions can lead you to become an expert on a topic, because most other people won't have the patience to learn everything you've learnt.

But for some people with Asperger's the teenage years are harder. If the people around you don't understand, you may feel isolated and be teased. It can make your life miserable.

Boyfriend/girlfriend issues can be tough for you, too. Non-Asperger teenagers learn social behaviours more quickly and naturally than you, and you may find it really hard to know what to say to a girl or boy you fancy.

Luckily, there are lots of strategies that can make a real difference to your life and happiness, and lots of potential benefits to having Asperger's.

SUGGESTED STRATEGIES
AND THINGS TO THINK ABOUT:

- My advice about boyfriends or girlfriends is the same for anyone: don't over-stress about it. Be patient; take your time; there's every chance of you finding happiness in a relationship if you want to. It's not something anyone can rush. And whoever you are, it's always best to be yourself – there are other people out there just like you.

- Whenever you want help with the things you find hard, ask for it. People don't always understand what's in your head, just as you don't always understand what's in theirs, so you have to make it clear.

- Don't let it get you down. You are not alone and although there is no cure for Asperger's there is a great deal of help and much more understanding than there was twenty years ago. I promise there are people who want to help.

- Remember that the teenage years are hard for many people and that my advice is: whatever your problems, talk to someone.

- One of the things other teenagers can find difficult about people with Asperger's is that they often behave more like adults than teenagers. That's good because soon you'll be an adult and be able to fit in much better!

Bereavement – losing a parent, brother, sister or friend

When someone you love dies, it rocks your life, whatever age you are. Grief is complicated, long and very hard at first. The world goes dark and you may panic, not knowing what to do, not believing you can ever feel happy again. If the death has been sudden, the shock can be huge. Grief can also involve anger, frustration, even guilt.

How does bereavement affect teenagers especially?

Younger children may be protected and wrapped up by the care of adults; they may also understand less and have less complicated feelings to deal with. Adults have their own support networks and their life experience to help them. A lot of the support seems to be focused on adults and often people don't know how to talk to teenagers about grief.

As a teenager, you may also find it hard to express what you need. Your feelings will be new for you and people may not understand them. Many adults themselves haven't had to deal with grief before.

People may assume you're feeling one thing when you're feeling something a bit different. If someone says, "You must be so shocked," when actually you're numb, angry or confused, it can be even more worrying, as you start to think, "Maybe there's something wrong with me if I'm not feeling the right things."

SUGGESTED STRATEGIES
AND THINGS TO THINK ABOUT:

- The best thing is to talk to an adult you're close to. But if for any reason you can't do that, or you'd rather not, follow my tips in *SECTION ONE* for finding another trusted adult.

- Don't worry if the person you want to talk to is also grieving. You can still talk to them. It might help them, too.

- There are special bereavement counsellors who will understand and value all of your feelings, however dark you think they are. They won't judge or condemn you or make you feel anything except understood and cared for. They can help you understand the different stages of grief and know that you will one day feel different. Whatever the circumstances of the death of the person you love – even the worst circumstances – bereavement counselling helps. It does.

- One very helpful thing is being able to talk to others the same age as you, who are going through the same things. The Grief Encounter website has some great ideas and ways of

230

getting in touch with them. For local groups aimed at bereaved young people, your doctor or library will have resources.

● When you feel that you will never be happy again, understand that this is not true. You just need help getting through this stage. It gets better. It really, really does.

What if your worries are nothing like the things I've mentioned?

Does this mean you're alone? No. Inside everyone's head are different thoughts and worries. It's common for teenagers to think that no one has the same dark thoughts or habits as they do, and even to worry that they are crazy. There will also be things I didn't have room for, like individual phobias, for example. All such anxieties will respond to the same strategies I've mentioned.

If your situation is genuinely exceptionally difficult or frightening, and isn't covered in this book, please talk to someone. Never feel alone. I know you aren't alone but you may need help to recognise that.

*"Be yourself. Don't change who you are
to please others/be part of the 'in' crowd.
Clothes/opinions seem important at school, but you
won't stay in touch with many school friends.
Take the subjects you like. Take time out for
yourself. Try and do something that you
enjoy/makes you smile every day."*

Nikki, adult

---

*"Find a few people who seem to have a good
life – it doesn't matter if they're personal
acquaintances or just people you see in TV
documentaries. Sometimes even fictional people will
do. You just need a few lives to hold in your mind
when everything is going wrong, to remind yourself
of the kind of grown-up you one day hope to be."*

Margo Lanagan, author

SECTION THREE

Dealing With and Preventing Symptoms of Stress

"Learn to meditate. Also, when you feel stressed or anxious, focus on your breath, accept how you feel right now and trust that neither the thing causing the stress nor your physical or emotional reaction to it will last for ever." **Liz Kessler, author**

In the previous section, I talked about the main worries you might have. And I suggested ways to help you worry less about them. But stress isn't something that vanishes when someone tells you not to worry. If only! So stress symptoms are something we have to watch out for and prevent if possible. You need to know how to be healthy in mind and body. Because mind and body are very closely connected and when the mind is stressed the body suffers.

233

These are useful tips for people of all ages. The skills you will learn in the next few pages can help you now and for the rest of your life.

I have divided them into things you can do for yourself (almost everything) and things you need special help with.

Things You Can Do For Yourself

There are lots of things we can each do to deal with stress. Small things and big things. We can prevent it becoming a problem. Or, when we see that it is becoming a problem, we can help it get better. The good thing about most of the tips I'm going to give you is that they're healthy, rewarding, easy and they work! Great tools for the rest of your life. But different ones may work for different people, so choose the ones you like the sound of.

Many of these tips involve treating yourself. Pleasure is not a luxury; it's a necessity. Whether it's a reward for hard work and effort, or a way to boost your health, pleasure is something your body and brain need.

Some of my suggestions are especially good for dealing with negative thoughts and emotions; others with stressful situations or periods during your life; and others are just good for a healthy body and mind, and can help prevent stress before it happens. Some are more practical and active, while others focus on changing thought processes. Choose the ones you like and which you think will work for you. Or try them all!

Ten-minute rewards

Some of the best advice I was ever given when I got stressed with work was to take regular breaks and to include a small reward.

Here are some ideas for ten-minute rewards. Ignore the things you don't think will work for you. And vary them.

- Have a drink (not alcohol). An occasional cup of tea or coffee is fine but remember that too much caffeine is bad for stress. A glass of water will help more than anything.
- Have a snack if you're hungry.
- Put on some loud music.
- Try one of the suggestions under **Using the senses to relax**. For example, light a scented candle.
- Meditate or practise mindfulness for a few minutes. (See below).
- Stroke a pet – it's known to lower the heart rate and boost mood.
- If you don't have a pet, hug a soft toy. Seriously.
- Go for a short walk or jog if the weather's nice.
- Lie on the grass and watch the clouds.

- Read a magazine.
- Message a friend – but only in a positive way.
- Eat a small amount of chocolate. (See below.)
- Do a crossword or Sudoku puzzle.

Daily half hour for *you*

This is similar to the point above, but it's a bigger thing. Set aside half an hour a day to do something just for you. Call it medicine for the soul.

Don't think of this as a reward – do it even if you don't feel you've done anything to deserve it. It is an important part of looking after yourself. Here are some ideas, but remember that it's important only to do what appeals to you:

- Visit a café. Take a book or meet a friend. Or just watch the people go by.
- Sit or lie in a comfortable position and practise deep breathing or one of the relaxation exercises I'll be describing later.
- Exercise. Go for a bike ride, swim, kick a football around. Dance or do aerobics to music turned up loud.
- One of the best ways to de-stress is to pamper yourself. Run a bath, light candles and have relaxing music in the background. Give yourself a manicure, pedicure or face mask.

- Read a book purely for pleasure.
- Do something creative. Take some photos, create a scrapbook of a recent holiday, make a birthday card for a friend, draw a picture.
- Do some creative writing – it's known to be a good stress reliever.
- Watch TV or a DVD. (But not if you've already been spending a long time staring at a screen.)
- Go to a park and just sit there. Try to notice things you've never noticed before.
- Do some cooking or baking.
- Go through all your clothes and get rid of everything you can't wear any more. Put some aside for charity and recycle the rest.
- Re-arrange the furniture in your room.
- Practise mindfulness or meditation. (See below.)

Breathe properly

I bet you think you know how to breathe. After all, you've been doing it all your life without thinking about it. Trouble is, most people don't breathe properly when they are under stress. When your body is faced with a threat or major stress, your heart rate increases and your breathing becomes fast and shallow. But that's only supposed to happen for a short time and your body should return to normal once the threat is over. But if you are under low-

SECTION THREE

level constant stress, including stress that you may hardly notice, your breathing will still be too shallow and you may never get full breaths of air.

You can test this now. Put one hand high on your chest (just under your neck) and one on your stomach. Carry on breathing just as you were before. Which hand is moving? If you're relaxed, it should be your stomach/ abdomen, not your chest. Your stomach should move out when you breathe in. Don't take huge long breaths, just slightly longer than usual.

So, that's the first thing: know what good breathing is. Second, practise something called 7/11: breathe in while you count to seven and out while you count to eleven. Do that a few times whenever you feel stressed and panicky. It's an instant help for emergencies.

A BREATHING EXERCISE

This is a technique anyone can learn quite easily. There are CDs or DVDs with exercises like this on, or you can download one you like from a website. (Please check that it is age-appropriate and legal.) There is one on my website, which I recorded myself and which is free.

1. Sit or lie somewhere comfortable, and make sure you won't be disturbed.
2. Take three or four deep breaths, in through the nose and out through the mouth. Make sure it's your stomach that moves, not your upper chest.
3. Focus on your feet and lower legs, making those muscles relax. Do this for 3-5 breaths, really thinking about the muscles and willing them to grow heavy and soft. (If you like, you can begin by tightening the muscles and then relaxing them.)
4. Let your focus move up your legs for a few breaths; then to your hips, abdomen and pelvis. Stay with each area for a few breaths.
5. Move your focus up through your stomach to your chest.
6. Then your fingers, hands, wrists, arms, all the way up to your shoulders.
7. Linger on your shoulders and the back of your neck, before continuing up the back of your head to the very top, and then finally down through your face, thinking about each bit of your face: forehead, eyes, cheeks, mouth and jaw. Do this in your own time.
8. Finish with a few more slow breaths and stay relaxed for as long as you want.

Exercise

Physical exercise is one of the very best stress-busting strategies. When we push our bodies and get out of breath and sweaty, we make several good things happen.

One is that we become physically healthier and fitter, improving our hearts and lungs. Another is that exercise releases chemicals called endorphins, which some people call "happy chemicals". Endorphins are the body's natural painkillers and they seem to help with both physical and mental pain. Even if you dislike actually doing the exercise, the feeling of satisfaction afterwards is fantastic. Many people start off not enjoying exercise but soon they find that it makes them feel so good that they begin to look forward to it and enjoy it more and more.

Whatever you choose, be careful. Have the right gear and, if you go running, don't go anywhere that puts you at risk. Always carry a phone if you go out. If you have any health problems, check with a doctor before you start exercising. And don't overdo it.

Suggestions for exercise:

- Find something you might like – classes, jogging, skating, cycling, football, for example.
- Get an exercise DVD and do it at home.
- Go for a fast walk. Walking is one of the best exercises and being outside has stress-relief benefits of its own.

- Dance crazily to loud music.
- Kick a ball against a wall.
- If you have a dog – or could borrow one – take it for a walk. Most dogs will love you forever if you do that and the act of caring for another creature is heart-lifting.
- Try yoga. Not only is it great exercise but it's specifically aimed at relaxation. It's also great for people (like me) who don't like running around. You can go to a class or get a DVD and do it at home without anyone seeing. A class is good, as the teacher can help you do it properly. But you'd only need to go to a few sessions before you could follow a DVD easily yourself.

Get outside

There's plenty of research suggesting that the human brain responds well to looking at the natural world, especially greenery and wide-open spaces. The brain's tendency to enjoy nature is called biophilia. Nature helps our mood and stress levels. It may even help creativity, though the research on that is not so clear. Some research has shown that walking in the woods helps heart rate, blood pressure and stress levels to fall; and it seems that patients may recover more quickly from surgery when they have a natural view. Based on all this, scientists have started to wonder whether even looking at pictures or photos of lovely views might help.

We also know that having enough daylight is important for mood. Lack of light increases your production of melatonin, making you sleepier. Some people are extra sensitive to this so they may be more depressed and low during the darker months. You might have heard of SAD (seasonal affective disorder). One of the treatments for SAD is light therapy, where patients have to sit for a certain amount of time each day with a special light. (Normal lights don't have the same effect because daylight is "whiter" than normal electric light. "Blue" light is also sometimes used. By the way, please check with a doctor before using a SAD light as there are a couple of medical conditions that may make it unsafe.)

So, getting outside every day is a really good idea and could make a big difference to you. It helps if you can find somewhere with a beautiful natural view. Looking out to sea or climbing a hill so that you have a big view would both be great if you can do that. If you live in a city, find the biggest and most beautiful park.

Why not suggest a trip to the seaside or countryside? Water, trees, mountains, rolling lawns: any of those will help de-stress you and lift your mood.

Also, just going somewhere new can refresh you and take your mind off worries. Try these:

● Go to the library. And, while you're there, see if

there are any classes or events that take your fancy.

- Visit a museum or art gallery, or go to the cinema or a concert.
- Be a tourist in your own town. Visit a tourist attraction or take a tourist bus.

Hobbies

If you have a hobby or anything that takes you away from your usual school and family world, you will be doing yourself and your brain a real favour. A hobby probably uses different parts of the brain from your schoolwork. It can give you a chance to meet different people and take your mind off whatever is worrying you. Here are some ideas:

- A sport that you maybe can't do at school. Skateboarding? Ice skating? Go to the gym?
- Join a new dance or fitness class.
- Music – if you already learn a musical instrument, don't give up now. Your brain is in a perfect state for becoming really good at it. How about writing your own songs? No one needs to hear them unless you want them to, but it could be a great outlet for your emotions. And you might find a hidden talent.
- Try making things – perhaps to sell. Do an internet search for "crafts for teens" and you'll find lots of

243

ideas of things you could learn to make and sell. You don't need a special talent, just an open mind. Look in markets and gift shops and see what sort of things people buy. Then you can sell your stuff on eBay or share a stall at a fair or carboot sale.

● Make a video. You don't need expensive equipment and lots of editing software is free and simple to use. The skills you learn could come in useful when someone else wants a video made, and it could be a chance to make some money.

● Reclaim old or broken objects and turn them into something else. For example, gardeners like growing plants in reclaimed cans, barrels, pots or anything that can hold soil. Again, you can do this just as a creative activity or turn it into a money-making opportunity. Car boot sales are great places both to find and sell things.

● Gardening. Is there any outside space you could use to grow things? Even just with some pots, you can try a lot of herbs, edible plants or flowers. You could even grow things to sell.

● Knitting and sewing. People of all ages and types enjoy knitting and find it relaxing. You don't only have to think about cardigans you'll never wear – check out patterns for knitting toys and weird things, too.

- Cookery – very easy to learn, and you don't need lessons. Your family will love you! (Well, maybe not at first...) Just buy a cookery book you like the look of or do an internet search for "teenagers cooking".
- Start a business. Again, there are lots of ideas for teenagers on the internet. Try searching "your teen business". Make sure your idea is legal and appropriate. And since you aren't trying to earn a living and you won't put a lot of money into it the normal stresses of running a business as an adult won't apply.
- Volunteering. Looking outside your own life and helping other people is a fantastic way of raising your self-esteem and forgetting your own worries. You can also learn a lot of good things about yourself, which might lead to a job later. Though there are strict rules about volunteering, there are still opportunities and, as always, the internet will show you things you can do in your area. Search "volunteering teenagers UK". For many things you'll need to be at least sixteen, but don't be put off: someone will welcome your help.
- Odd jobs for family and neighbours. Cleaning cars, weeding paths, babysitting, watering gardens, housework: all these things can be relaxing and enjoyable, and help you earn a bit of cash.

Readaxation – relax with a book

Readaxation is a word I made up. It means "reading to relax" and really works. Reading fiction takes you into another world or another person's head and allows you to forget your own worries. Or, if you choose to read a book where the characters have the same worries it can sometimes help you work through your own stresses. And if you prefer non-fiction, that's equally valuable for stress relief. It's about reading for pleasure, not for schoolwork.

The best person to suggest ideal books for you is your school librarian. If you want to read about a particular issue or theme, tell them and say whether you want a funny book, a scary one or whatever.

A word of warning: sometimes it helps to read about someone going through the same thing as you, but it *can* make you feel worse, depending on your situation. For example, if you are feeling down, or if you have been self-harming, reading a book about that *might* make you feel worse. If you are not sure whether a particular book would suit you, talk to your school librarian.

Express yourself in writing

Many teenagers enjoy expressing their emotions in creative writing. I used to write very gloomy poetry. The gloomier the better, as far as I was concerned. It was over the top emotionally but I loved the power of the words and loved it if I could make myself cry. One day, my English teacher decided that my poetry sounded worryingly depressed and I remember looking at her as though she was mad. I wasn't depressed – I was just angsty and full of emotions that I wanted to express.

No one has to read your writing if you don't want them to. But it can be an effective way of expressing your feelings safely. It doesn't have to be about you: if you prefer, you can imagine yourself as someone else and write a made-up story, or a story that looks made-up but has some elements of your own feelings in it. In fact, there's evidence that putting your experiences into someone else's voice – for example, by saying "she felt" instead of "I feel" – helps us process bad emotions or memories.

If you want to do it, do it. If it makes you feel worse, stop doing it. It really is that simple.

If you enjoy it, you could enter a writing competition or contribute to magazines. That's how many published writers start. So, you're not only expressing yourself: you're practising your writing skills, just as a musician practises musical skills. Go for it!

Express yourself in music or art

Creating music or art can have a positive effect on stress,

too. As with writing, it takes practice before you can produce something satisfying, but it's a very good way of letting out emotions and preventing the bad effects of stress.

Food and drink

A healthy diet doesn't just affect your body but how you feel and how your brain works. It helps you be fit and well and may also affect your mood. You can help control stress by making sure your diet includes certain foods and drinks and doesn't include others.

However, let me warn you about something. On the internet you will find lots of articles saying "research shows" that a particular food or supplement is good for mood or depression or whatever. It's usually hard to know how good that research is so you need to be careful what you believe.

One thing I am sure of is that including a reasonable number of the foods I recommend below in your diet will have a positive effect. (Unless you are allergic to any of them...) And the act of choosing a healthy, wide-ranging and balanced diet is a positive one.

But even if a food is especially brilliant for your brain, it doesn't mean you should have too much of it. If you only ate blueberries, for example, it wouldn't be good for you. Moderation is best, and a varied diet.

Things I recommend:

- **Vitamin B** There are various B vitamins but there's no need to separate them as it's best to eat all of them. Look for these foods: most fruit and veg – especially peas, spinach and broccoli – eggs, many fortified cereals (it will say on the packet if they contain B vits), milk and rice. If you really can't eat a range of those foods, you might take a "vitamin B complex" supplement, but it's best to get your vitamins from food, so check with an adult first.

- **Chocolate** Yes! There's now a lot of evidence suggesting that chocolate is good for mood and stress. BUT a) it needs to be dark chocolate and b) too much is bad for you because it contains a lot of sugar and will wreck your blood sugar levels, making you feel worse. So, go for dark chocolate and just give yourself a little bit each day. You can tell how dark a chocolate is by looking at the packet and seeing what percentage of cocoa solids it contains. 70% or higher is best.

- **Omega 3 oils** Found in oily fish, such as salmon, mackerel and sardines. It's not clear how well Omega 3 supplements work, so it's advisable to get the nutrients direct from food itself.

- **Brazil nuts** A good source of selenium, which is believed to be important for mood; you only need to eat three nuts to get the daily amount you need.

Other nuts are also good ways to fuel your brain.

- **Oats** Try porridge, flapjacks and anything with whole oats. They release energy slowly and help keep your blood sugar levels steady. If your blood sugar levels rocket up and down, it can make you anxious, jittery and unable to concentrate.

- **Bananas** Clever little foods, bananas. They contain a load of good things, such as tryptophan and vitamin B6, which are supposed to help mood and sleep. And they are a great source of potassium.

- **Lentils** They have some of the same effects as bananas. They also help boost iron levels, and that's very important for mood and energy.

- **Relaxing teas** You'll find lots of fruit or herbal teas in supermarkets or health food shops. Obviously, look for those that say they are for sleep or relaxation. They will usually contain ingredients such as passiflora, lavender, hops, chamomile and valerian, which are well-known for their calming properties.

- **Water** Because it helps your brain work well (and if your brain isn't working well that's stressful!).

Things to be careful about or avoid:

- **Caffeine** There's nothing wrong with the odd cup of coffee (or tea, because normal tea also has caffeine in it) but too much can make you jittery and make your heart race. It can also affect your blood sugar levels in a bad way.

- **Alcohol** Alcohol is a very bad way to deal with stress, even though one of the first things that happens when you drink it is that you feel relaxed. The relaxed feeling soon passes and more negative feelings, including depression or anger, can set in. If people use alcohol to deal with stress, the risk of addiction is very high.

- **Too much sugar** Most foods contain natural sugar but when you consume too much added sugar (and many manufactured foods have a lot of hidden sugar) it makes your energy levels shoot up and down. This is incredibly unrelaxing and stops your brain working well. So, don't drink sugary drinks – pretty much all fizzy drinks – as it's the fastest way to get a sugar high followed by a sugar crash.

Herbal remedies

People have used herbs for stress for thousands of years – at least since 3000 BC – and many people think that because they are "just herbs" they are safe. The truth is that they can work, but they can have side-effects and react with other medicines. Also, adverts for herbal remedies sometimes make claims that simply haven't been proven. So, I don't recommend that you take any herbal medicines without asking your doctor or pharmacist.

But it's hard to imagine a herbal tea causing you harm as long as you drink a sensible amount. Some teas are labelled as being good for stress, or to help sleep, and I see no reason not to try these, unless, of course, you are allergic to any of the ingredients. I have one that I drink each night. I can't say whether it helps, but I like it and it costs very little.

Laughter

Possibly the best stress-reliever there is! Laughter has genuine benefits for mood. Apparently, even pretending to laugh – in other words forcing a fake laugh and creasing your face into a grin – has the right effect. When you use those facial muscles it is supposed to help release endorphins into your blood. There are even things called "laughter yoga classes", where everyone sits there and laughs!

You don't need to attend a class. There are plenty of easy and obvious ways to have a laugh:

- Keep a stock of your favourite funny movies and put one on when you need a mood boost.
- And your favourite comedians – there are usually clips online.
- YouTube and other video sites have an endless supply of hilarious clips. Try searching for the following phrases: "goats that scream like humans", "laughing babies", "babies eating lemons", "talking

252

animals" and "dancing ponies". But don't get side-tracked by the darker side – laughing at someone who is genuinely hurt won't help you.

One problem with feeling really down, though, is that you may not even think about laughter. Someone may need to remind you. Also, a symptom of depression is that you may find that nothing makes you laugh. If this is how you feel for more than a few days, please see a doctor.

Releasing anger and tension

If you're feeling angry or the stress is about to boil over, here are some tips for letting your anger out safely:
- Go somewhere where you can scream. Or do it into your pillow.
- Kick a ball.
- Punch a pillow or mattress.
- Get a big lump of Blu-Tack or plasticine and squeeze it. Or a stress ball, if you have one.
- Do twenty press-ups.
- Tear up newspaper.

Music therapy

Music can make a big difference to mood and stress levels. It's an almost-instant fix. But you need to think about what

SECTION THREE

music will be best because different types of music will have different results.

Here are some suggestions:

- Try choosing music that is the opposite of how you're feeling. So, if you're feeling jangled or angry or hyper, choose calming, slow music. If you are feeling sad and down, try faster, exciting music. Sometimes people play sad songs when they feel sad. If that helps you, fine, but I recommend focusing on music that makes you feel good.

- Think about how you use music when you are working. Everyone is different and some people work better with music and others without. Some like their music loud and with a strong beat, others prefer it soft and soothing. There are no rules. Do what works for you.

- Use music to block out annoying noises from the rest of your house.

- Music can also help block out annoying thoughts.

- Don't ignore classical music – there's as much variety in it as in any type of music. Some you might like; some you'll find boring. I'm no expert but as examples of two incredibly different pieces, try Beethoven's 5th Symphony and *The Lark Ascending* by Vaughan Williams. You might hate both of them but you have to agree they are both different and could have a very different effect on your mood.

Using the senses to relax

We've been given five senses but we often charge through life without thinking about them. One way to focus your thoughts more positively and to calm down a stressed mind is to focus on your senses in specific ways. Here are some suggestions:

- Use colours to change your mood. (See **Colour therapy and coloured breathing**.)
- Get three foods you like – strawberries, bananas, chocolate, mint, crisps, honey, lime, for example – and try one at a time, really slowly, thinking about the taste as it travels round your mouth.
- Light a scented candle or have a scented bath.
- Buy (or make) wind chimes for your window.
- Make sure you can see something nice when you're at your desk – the view from the window or, if you haven't got one, a picture of a beautiful view.
- Have music playing – but properly listen to it.
- Give yourself a hand or foot massage. Warm your hands and then systematically rub and squeeze each part of your hands and feet, gently pulling each finger and toe. Focus on each part as you massage it, using as much pressure as is comfortable.
- Aromatherapy involves the use of certain oils to induce certain moods. I'm not making claims for

any science behind it but if you enjoy the smells they are likely to have a positive effect, so go for it. Oils that are supposed to be good for relaxation include lavender, camomile, neroli, orange, bergamot and ylang-ylang. You can put a couple of drops in a bath (though not all oils are suitable for skin so check on the bottle) or put them on a room burner with a tea light.

Colour therapy and coloured breathing

Different colours seem to affect us in different ways and you can sometimes change your mood by the clever use of colours around you. But it is hard for teenagers to control the colour of their surroundings, unless you fancy redecorating your room, which is actually not a bad idea. So, the good (and slightly crazy-sounding) thing is that "coloured breathing" lets you *imagine* certain colours and affect your mood like that. I know this sounds weird, but it works for lots of people and I'm a great believer in "if it works, do it".

A very simple version goes like this: breathe in while thinking of a calming colour (blue – the most beautiful blue you can think of, like a swimming-pool or summer sky) and breathe out while thinking of the colour red, which is often an angry colour. So, you imagine yourself breathing away the anger.

Some people suggest much more complicated ways of using colours to change mood. If you are interested, you'll find a link in the resources at the back and you can investigate on the internet. I did and a lot of it sounds pretty strange to me, but some parts sound worth trying.

Controlling your thoughts

Many different therapies can help you control your mind so that you aren't overwhelmed by intrusive, negative thoughts. The thoughts that buzz around your head have a huge effect on how you feel. If you have sad thoughts too often, or blame yourself for things, or feel angry about yourself or other people, it can overwhelm you and stop you having positive thoughts. Also, negative thoughts are often wrong; you may be blaming yourself for no reason. We are often not very kind to ourselves.

I have collected the main "thought control" exercises that you can do for yourself. Some are also used by therapists and so, if you have any of the treatments that require professional help, you may come across them then in more detail.

Deliberate daydreaming

Having positive fantasy daydreams can be very uplifting, and they might continue in your sleeping dreams. Once you've thought of a dream scenario, something you'd love to happen, you can conjure up this daydream any time your thoughts seem to be turning negative. It can also help you get to sleep or at least switch off the worries that are keeping you awake.

Visualisation

This involves picturing a beautiful place where you feel safe and happy. In my case it's a tropical beach, with white sands and winds whispering in the palm trees. I'm on my own but I feel totally safe. I'm the perfect temperature. The colours are white, yellow and vivid blue with some green. And I can transport myself there in an instant. Your place might be completely different. It's a very helpful technique for calming stressed or sleepless minds. And you can combine it with other relaxation exercises and deep breathing.

Meditation

Meditation is the art of going into very deep relaxation and focusing your thoughts on a specific thing. It needs practice. It lets you block out everything else. You go into a relaxation so deep that if you were lying down you might fall asleep, so people usually do it sitting up in a cross-legged position. It's popular in lots of Eastern religions. Tibetan monks, for example, are experts in meditation and mindfulness and can achieve great calm. Research suggests that their regular meditation changes their brains to a state of greater relaxation even when they aren't actually meditating.

Mindfulness

Mindfulness is a type of meditation and is very popular. It's about deliberately focusing on the present moment and accepting it without judgement. So, it's the opposite of blocking intrusive thoughts because in mindfulness you are supposed to let them in, but then let them out. Ask your school about the "mindfulness in schools" programme and you can easily find details on the internet.

Here is a simple version of this type of meditation which you can try yourself. You will get more benefit if you practise every day.

1. Sit comfortably and think about your breathing. Notice the breath coming in and out. Notice your thoughts coming and going and make no judgement about them.

2. If you wish, you can think of a word and keep repeating it in your head. Best if it's a made up word. Or you could try "Ommmmm". If that makes you want to laugh, again just notice that thought and let it go. It doesn't matter.

3. Notice all the feelings in your body. Focus on each part of your body in turn.

4. Think about each of your senses. What can you see (behind closed eyes), smell, hear, taste, touch? Don't

try to describe them; just notice them.

5. What are you feeling? Name the emotions but don't judge them as good or bad. So, if you feel nervous, notice that; if you feel sad, notice that. Say, in your head, "nervousness, sadness," and let them pass.

6. Are there noises outside? Outside your room? Outside the house? Just notice them, without wondering about them. Don't let your thoughts linger on anything and don't let yourself begin to think about the past or the future. If your thoughts seem to want to go in that direction, steer them back to what you are feeling now.

7. If a "bad" thought comes into your mind, something you are disappointed or ashamed about, forgive yourself. Let it pass through your head and leave.

Here is a way to use music for mindfulness:

1. Sit somewhere comfortable where you won't be disturbed

2. Zone into the music, noticing things you hadn't noticed before: the bass line, individual instruments, the parts that are quieter or louder.

3. Notice the music flowing through your body, what it's doing to you, what emotions it's creating.

4. Think about the musicians playing or singing.

5. Let the music sweep you away. If any other

thoughts come into your head, notice them but let them go.

Autogenics

Autogenics is a bit like meditation, too, except that you focus on slowing your heart rate by thinking about it. You start by getting into a relaxed state, using the breathing exercise I described earlier, and then you try to will your heart rate to slow as your muscles feel heavier and heavier. People who practise this can make their blood pressure reduce as well as their heart rate.

Dealing with intrusive thoughts

Do you have a negative thought or fear that keeps attacking you? Perhaps you can't get rid of it, or it disappears but keeps coming back. Sometimes you may think it's driving you mad. Perhaps you go over and over it, constructing unlikely but horrible situations that feel real. If this happens a lot and is really spoiling your life, you may consider having some professional treatment (see later) but there are also very useful things you can try yourself. I often have negative recurring thoughts and I've become much better at getting rid of them but I wish I'd had the skills earlier.

Here are some suggestions:

- Say No. Every time the intrusive thought tries to take over, just say No. You can either say this in your head or (if no one is near!) say it aloud. You may have to keep doing this over a period of days. And it may come back later but you'll be able to deal with it again.

● Replace it with a positive thought. For example, the ideas mentioned in **Deliberate Daydreaming** and **Visualisation** above. If you have a mental picture of a beautiful, safe place, you can quickly think of that instead of the nasty negative thought that's trying to invade your mind.

● Distract it with another activity. Something you can start immediately, without preparation: draw a picture, read a magazine or book, play a computer game, make a list of things you'd like for your birthday or do one of the thinking positive exercises below.

Be positive

Negative thinking becomes a habit and it can be hard to break. Far too many of us focus on the negative aspects of ourselves. It's one of the main things that therapists have to deal with. Negative thinking can stop you achieving your potential and it certainly stops you being happy. It can make you have a completely false idea about yourself and not see yourself as others see you.

Here are some tips for positive thinking:

- Make a list of all the good things about your life that you can think of. Even really tiny things, such as the fact that you could eat your favourite food if you wanted to. Don't forget to include being glad about bad things that *haven't* happened to you.
- Remember there are things about your life that could be worse. If that doesn't seem obvious at first, think about people your age in countries with civil wars and starvation.
- Look ahead and imagine a time when your current worries have gone and you have more control over your life.
- Try the ideas under **Laughter**. The physical act of laughing can flip your negative thoughts away.
- Do a good deed for someone. What we do affects our brains. If you do some good things, you set up good thoughts in your brain and will feel better about yourself. Even saying something nice to someone will make you feel better. So, tell your friend you like their shoes or compliment your mum or dad.
- Do a good deed for yourself. You are a good person going through some hard times and you deserve a reward. Doing something positive for yourself will help set up a positive thought.

Cognitive Bias Modification

Many anxious and stressed people have a tendency to look on the negative side of life, to worry about unnecessary things. Obviously, so do people with depression. There's some new research into this and one of the interesting results is a possible treatment called cognitive bias modification. It's early stages yet and isn't widely available but, basically, it involves some simple computer exercises to get you to focus on happy faces instead of angry or sad ones. There are already some apps but I can't vouch for how good they are. As I say, it's early days, but, if it does turn out to work, it could be hugely beneficial for many people.

Until then, the more you can make yourself think, say and watch positive things, the better. Each time a negative thought comes along, turn it inside out so that you find yourself saying and thinking the opposite. Treat it like an exercise or a game and you'll soon find it becomes easier and more natural. You could be creating your very own cognitive bias modification tool!

Choose your friends

Who you hang out with can make a real difference to your mood. I've heard people described as "balcony or basement" people. Balcony people take you up to a high place and show you the view; basement people drag you down and stop you seeing the possibilities of life.

I'm not suggesting you dump all your friends who don't live up to your ideals but I am suggesting you think about which people make you feel good when you are with them. Which people let you express yourself? Which are non-judgemental? Stick with them.

Guardian angel

I made this up! It involves thinking of someone who always gives you good advice, someone you trust. It could be someone you actually know or it could be an imagined, ideal person. When you have negative thoughts or are worried or upset, ask yourself what this guardian angel would say if they knew you were worrying. Would they say, "Yeah, actually, you're right to worry"? No, of course not! That's what you are saying, but you have warped, negative thoughts which could make you ill. Listen to your guardian angel. That's the voice of wisdom.

Call on them any time worries are weighing you down or negative thoughts are getting in the way.

If you like, imagine what I would say to you.

Get a good night's sleep

I talked about sleep problems earlier in this book, so you know how important sleep is to a healthy mind and body.

265

If you can get an extra twenty minutes a night this will really help. So, why not start your bedtime routine half an hour or so earlier tonight? It could make a real difference.

There are lots of ways to improve your sleep patterns and fall asleep more quickly. Most of the advice is about what you should do and not do during the hour before you want to feel sleepy. Sometimes this advice is called "sleep hygiene".

Things to avoid in the hour before sleep:
- Bright lights
- Caffeine
- Alcohol
- Heavy meals
- Food, snacks or drinks high in sugar
- Loud, fast music
- Computers, TV, DVDs, electronic games, phones, tablets, anything involving the internet
- Exercise that raises your heart rate
- Excitement
- Arguments and stressful conversations

Things that help in the hour before sleep:
- Dim lights
- Herbal or fruit teas, or a warm milky drink
- Quiet music
- Reading

- Writing a diary
- Making a list of things to take to school in the morning
- Pottering around, doing anything unstressful
- A shower or bath, especially with lavender oil

Next, you need to create a routine to trick your brain into new habits and make it think, "Ah, this means it's time to sleep." The brain responds well to new routines and a new habit can form quite quickly.

Here's an example of a routine, but you need to create your own. If you do this for a few nights in a row, your brain will recognise the signals and start to feel sleepy.

1. Make yourself a relaxing drink (see ideas above) and, if you're hungry, a small snack.
2. Dim the lights and shut the curtains in your bedroom. Turn off all electronic machines.
3. Play some quiet, slow music.
4. Tidy all your clothes away (your parents are going to love me!) and get everything ready for the morning.
5. Have a bath or shower and clean your teeth. (If you've finished your snack, obviously...)
6. Get into your nightclothes and get into bed.
7. Write a diary and/or read a book or magazine that you're enjoying – not a school book. If you hate reading, you could do a puzzle or make a list, or

just shut your eyes and have a daydream.

8. When you feel sleepy, turn the light off and carry on thinking about the book you were reading or the daydream you were having.

Extra tips for improving sleep:

- Keep a sleep diary. See whether your worst nights' sleep coincide with a big meal late at night, particular foods, doing heavy exercise, working too late, or something else. Then you know what to avoid.

- Most people sleep better at night if they haven't had naps during the day. So, if you're tempted to have a nap at weekends, try not to. If you do and you find you can still sleep well at night, that's fine, but sleeping during the day is generally not recommended unless you're ill.

- Try not to compensate for a bad night by sleeping in late or going to bed too early the next night.

- Do you have a big worry that is keeping you awake? If it's something you haven't been worrying about much during the day, tell yourself that this is because it's not actually an important worry – you're only thinking about it now because it's night-time.

- Are you worrying about something that you can't actually do anything about right now? Tell yourself that worrying is not going to help. Try writing the worry on a piece of paper and putting it somewhere in your room to deal with in the morning. This doesn't work for everything but it's a good skill to practise. We can control our minds more than we think. It takes practice and belief.

● Remember that you can manage on less sleep than you imagine. Also, just twenty minutes extra makes a big difference.

What About Professional Help?

If all the things I've already suggested are not enough to help you, you may need help from a professional in one of the range of therapies that exist for every sort of anxiety or mental problem. Your doctor is the best person to advise you and should always be the first person to talk to if you want help.

Some therapies are available on the NHS, which means they have been approved by NICE, the committee that decides what treatments are allowed to be free on the NHS. But some are not. Most are approved only for certain conditions, so your doctor has to decide if you qualify. NICE looks at evidence and research and decides which things are worth public money.

Treatments that are not approved by NICE could work,

but the committee does not believe there is enough proof of their value. Some psychiatrists or doctors might say that there's no harm in trying those alternative therapies, but others might say the opposite. My advice is trust your doctor or the specialist you've been referred to.

If you and your parents are looking for a therapist (assuming your doctor has agreed that it is worth trying) it's really important to check their qualifications. Get a recommendation from the organisation that regulates the therapy you are interested in. It is essential that you have a good therapist, someone who is used to working with young people, and someone you get along with.

Even though your GP might agree that a particular therapy could work for you, if the therapy isn't approved by NICE, they will not be able to recommend a therapist, only give you general advice.

Your therapist should have a DBS certificate (Disclosure and Barring Service) before working with young people. As an extra precaution, I recommend you always have a trusted adult waiting outside the treatment room for you.

Sometimes, the therapist could be excellent but you just don't get along with her or him. You might, for example, feel patronised. This may just be because you are feeling hostile and angry, so I would recommend being patient at first. But if you really don't think you can get along with this therapist – or with this therapy – just tell your parents or trusted adult. You haven't failed and nor has the therapist.

How to get treatment

Whatever is wrong with you, start by seeing your GP. They have guidelines which allow them to prescribe certain treatments. Some GP practices have their own counselling services, which may be free, or they may be able to advise you in other ways.

If your GP can't help you or if you want a therapy they can't advise about, an adult can contact the organisation that regulates the therapy (see the resources section) for approved therapists in your area. Your local library or Yellow Pages will also have suggestions and then you can check with those organisations whether the therapists are recognised.

So, if you happen to want a particular treatment that's not the one listed as being best for your symptoms, your GP cannot give it to you but may be able to give you other helpful advice.

With therapies that are not regulated by the NHS, it is essential to take care: don't waste money and time or risk making yourself ill.

THE MOST COMMON TREATMENTS

Cognitive Behavioural Therapy (CBT)

CBT is widely used and recommended, with a great deal of evidence to back it up. It is available on the NHS for some

271

conditions, though availability may depend on where you live.

CBT is a "talking" therapy and is used to treat all sorts of negative thinking patterns. It can be very helpful for depression, anxiety, panic, eating disorders, addictions, self-harming and obsessive disorders.

CBT doesn't delve into your past and try to find causes, though sometimes that might happen during the conversation. So, if your problems are due to something traumatic from your past, or to something to do with your family, CBT on its own may not be enough, because it only focuses on your symptoms, rather than possible causes.

It focuses on what you are going through now and how you can learn to change it. You will be given mental exercises to practise between sessions.

You would usually see a therapist once a week or fortnight, over several months. The therapist starts by discussing your problems and how you think about yourself and the world, finding out exactly what your negative thought patterns and beliefs are. She or he breaks down the whole situation into small points, tackling the underlying problems. Then the therapist works with you to show you how to change your harmful thoughts, often with practical exercises.

Your therapist will have seen the same problems many times, although each person is different. However, its success very much does depend on the individual therapist and if you happen not to like the one you are given it's really important to tell your parents or whoever is caring for you. But do give it time, as it is not a quick fix.

Although it's well known and successful, CBT is not a magic pill, so it does need commitment and cooperation from you. It doesn't always work quickly, so you need to be patient. If you have to go privately, it will probably be expensive, because it usually takes time to re-shape your thinking.

For further advice, see the resources section under **CBT**. Websites that focus on specific problems such as eating disorders or bereavement may also lead you to CBT-type therapies.

Eye Movement Desensitisation and Reprocessing (EMDR)
I must say I was really surprised to discover that this treatment is available on the NHS, but it is and that means that NICE have checked out the research and decided that there is enough evidence that it works for certain conditions and that it is valuable. It is used to deal with post-traumatic stress disorder, including a really tough childhood that perhaps contained abuse or neglect. An advantage is that treatment can be quite short, too.

EMDR is based on the fact that when we are asleep we go through a stage called REM sleep, which stands for "rapid eye movement". The theory is that this rapid eye movement is there for a reason: to heal traumatic memories by allowing us to process them in the correct parts of the brain. And the idea is that sometimes our brains fail to deal with the traumatic memories properly. So, EMDR involves getting you to think about upsetting memories while following a moving object (such as the therapist's finger) to create rapid eye movement. Afterwards, you tell the therapist whether your thoughts changed during the REM session. The hope is that your memory then becomes less upsetting, as your brain begins to process it in the right parts.

Yes, I know. It sounds like magic. But, as I say, it's an approved treatment, even if the reasons for its effectiveness are unclear. So, if your GP thinks this might help you, you can get the treatment free on the NHS.

A word of warning: it can be upsetting to go through those bad memories.

Hypnotherapy

Hypnotherapy is not available on the NHS for most conditions, but many people find it extremely useful to treat a range of problems, particularly fears and anxieties, panic, low self-esteem and obsessive habits. Although you will have to pay for it, you might only need a very small number of sessions (sometimes only one or two) so it doesn't need to cost much. You may be given a person-alised CD to listen to at home and often you'll be taught to use the techniques on yourself.

A hypnotherapist aims to get you into a state of deep relaxation and then works on your subconscious thoughts, the ones you don't even know you have. You will be fully awake and in control and the hypnotherapist will not be able to make you do anything you don't want to do.

You can also buy hypnotherapy CDs or download them from approved sites on the internet. Please ask an adult before doing this, as some of them may be rubbish and some may be inappropriate for young people. I have also heard of people having hypnotherapy over the phone and this helped one person I know overcome a phobia.

Neuro-linguistic Programming (NLP)

Neuro-linguistic Programming has some similarities to CBT but is not available on the NHS. Like CBT, it tries to help our minds and thoughts be healthier, by showing us positive and useful ways of thinking. NLP studies how our thoughts affect our brains, making us behave in certain ways and, like CBT, it encourages us to think in a more healthy and useful way.

But NLP is not just a therapy for dealing with problems. Sportspeople, businesspeople, teachers, families and many others use it to understand themselves and others better. In fact, NLP is based on watching how successful, happy people think and trying to apply that to anyone who wants to be more successful and happy.

275

Because it's not available on the NHS, you will have to pay for private sessions. The good news is that most people don't need many sessions: between two and five is normal.

You can also learn Neuro-linguistic Programming techniques using a book. I recommend borrowing one from the library so that you can take time to make sure it feels right for you. You don't want a book that goes into too much detail about the theory, just one that has clear exercises and learning points. As well as checking out the ones I've mentioned at the back of this book, do an internet search for "NLP for teenagers" and you will quickly find interesting resources, including at least one book.

Biofeedback and neurofeedback

These treatments are not available on the NHS. Biofeedback (focusing on any parts of the body) and neurofeedback (a specific type of biofeedback focusing on the brain) involve finding out how your body is reacting and then trying to change those reactions, using concentration and mind control.

For example, if you had a machine that was measuring your heart rate so that you could hear it or see the patterns on a screen, you might try to relax your body; then, when you saw your heart rate slow on the monitor, that would show you that you were doing the right thing and you would then keep doing it, watching your heart rate slow down.

Since the techniques require machinery, full-scale biofeedback can be expensive. There are some simple gadgets that you can find yourself, however. For example, there are heat-reactive plastic dots, which you wear on your skin, and stress cards, which you hold in your hand – the dot or card changes colour according to how stressed you are. (It does this by reacting to skin temperature, because when you're stressed the blood rushes away from the skin, making you colder to touch.)

The ones I've tried have been variable in accuracy. They can be hard to read and often seem to react more to the temperature in the room than to my stress levels. But they are cheap and useful in that they make you think about relaxing.

To be honest, what I've seen offered in terms of treatment or gadgets has been pretty varied, so my advice is always to check carefully any treatment or therapy you plan to use. As with everything, the more expensive something is, the more you'd want to check it out.

Psychotherapy

Psychotherapy is the word that covers any kind of therapy for the mind rather than other parts of the body. But when most people say it they tend to mean the therapies that psychiatrists and psychologists are trained to use, not more alternative things such as laughter therapy or music therapy.

Psychoanalysis

Psychoanalysis is a very specific type of psychotherapy, which looks into things that have happened in your early life, which you might have forgotten about. Psychoanalysts believe that the patterns laid down by things that we experienced long before we can remember have hidden effects on our later emotions; they believe that when we see and understand these patterns, we can have better control over our lives.

Psychoanalysis is sometimes available on the NHS. You will be treated by a therapist with special training in child and adolescent psychoanalysis.

Medicines, such as anti-depressants

Only your GP can decide whether these are necessary or right for you. The guidelines have changed in recent years, after scientists discovered that the way many drugs work on adolescents' brains is different. Some anti-depressants, for example, have been shown to have suicidal effects on young people and only a doctor or properly qualified medical practitioner should ever recommend or prescribe them.

So, I cannot and would not give you any advice about this other than: see your doctor. If you are on anti-depressants and you find the side-effects difficult, you must see your doctor immediately. But don't stop taking them until they tell you to. If you come off anti-depressants too quickly, you may experience serious problems.

Conclusion

I learnt something interesting while writing this book: that dwelling on sad and stressful things makes us sad and stressed. As I was writing and researching, I was constantly coming across descriptions of symptoms and feeling hugely sympathetic for people going through difficult times. And, because I kept mentioning aspects of stress on my blog and asking people to tell me their experiences, I was being overwhelmed by some really sad stories. Parents and teenagers were talking to me about their experiences of bullying, cyber-bullying, depression, panic attacks, their feelings of anger and fear and pressure. Teenagers were telling me about symptoms or behaviours they thought meant they were alone, weird, crazy.

And, as this went on, I found myself feeling more and more down. That made me realize the truth of one of my earlier suggestions: that laughter is the best medicine. Because if we are constantly bombarded by sad or negative thoughts and allow them to take over, they grind us down and make us feel even more sad and negative. And the opposite is true, too.

I'm fortunate not to be going through a period of great stress; I'm strong and well and I know how to look after myself. But this wasn't always the case. I didn't find it at all easy being a teenager; in fact, I found it really difficult. I was anxious, confused, often angry, definitely not in control.

People change. I did. I wish I'd known I would. I wish I'd had a book like this to reassure me about the things I thought but couldn't say.

Too many teenagers feel alone inside their heads. Too many find the transition from protected child to independent adult tough and dark and stormy. Maybe not all the time, but sometimes. I wrote this book for you.

Too many adults don't know how to prevent and heal the negative effects of stress. Perhaps they can learn from this book.

I want you all to be strong and well and to look after yourselves. Some of you will find it harder than others; some of you have tougher lives than others. Life won't always be perfect; sometimes it will throw things at you that will be hard or seem impossible to deal with. But you can do more than you think, survive more than you fear, thrive more than you believe. Every challenge can make you stronger, every day you grow new cells, new skills. It's your brain, your body, your life. Look after them, now you know how.

APPENDIX:

Resources

These are merely starting points for each topic. There are lots of other great resources out there and new websites and books appearing all the time. If you don't know how to use the internet safely, ask for help.

Please be aware that the content of any of the sites or pages listed below may change. I found them useful when I looked at them but you can use your own judgement.

A word of warning: you're all at different stages and ready for different information. If anything listed here makes you feel uncomfortable, choose something else.

There is lots of help on my own website and blog **www.nicolamorgan.com** and you can get your teachers and parents to sign up to my free "My Brain Sane" newsletter, which has lots of up-to-date resources.

General help for young people

To find your local health clinic specially for young people, internet search the phrase "young people's clinic local" and then your post code.

www.childline.org.uk There is an online instant chatroom on the website or you can call 0800 1111 in the UK. It will not show up on your bill and calls are free. You can use a pretend name if you want. It is totally confidential and they will only tell anyone else if your life is in immediate danger.

www.itsalright.org

www.kidshealth.org/teen

www.mentalhealth.org.uk follow link for "Supporting emotional health and wellbeing in schools"

www.mind.org.uk

www.mindfull.org Mindfull is a service aimed at 11-17 year-olds. It's a spin-off from Beat Bullying and has counselling for self-harming but also looks at many other problems.

www.nhs.uk for treatments available on the NHS near you

au.reachout.com

somazone.com.au Somazone is an Australian site where young people can ask questions about anything that worries them.

www.Youthnet.org

Specific issues

ABUSE/RESPECT (EG IN RELATIONSHIPS)

thisisabuse.direct.gov.uk

www.respectyourself.info

ACNE

www.nhs.uk/Conditions/Acne

ADHD/ADD

www.livingwithadhd.co.uk and click on "Are you a teenager?"

aacap.org/cs/root/facts_for_families/children_who_cant_pay_
attention/attention_deficit_hyperactivity_disorder

www.youngminds.org.uk and search "ADHD"

ALCOHOL OR DRUGS

www.drinkaware.co.uk

pbs.org/inthemix/educators/lessons/alcohol1/factsheet.html

www.talktofrank.com

www.nhs.uk/Livewell/teenboys/Pages/Truthaboutdrugs.aspx

ANOREXIA – see eating disorders

ANXIETY AND PANIC

www.mind.org.uk under "Information and Support", choose "A–Z Mental Health" and select "Anxiety and Panic Attacks"

www.anxietyuk.org.uk

AUTISM AND ASPERGER'S

www.autism.org.uk

www.teenagerswithaspergers.com

community.autism.org.uk

Books: *Born on a Blue Day* by Daniel Tammet

Animals in Translation by Temple Grandin

BEREAVEMENT

www.griefencounter.org.uk

www.facingbereavement.co.uk/talking-teens-about-death. html

BLUSHING

www.nhs.uk/Conditions/Blushing

BULIMIA – see eating disorders

BULLYING

www.beatbullying.org

www.bullying.co.uk

www.nhs.uk/Livewell/Bullying

www.kidscape.org.uk

www.stopbullying.gov

www.inspiremykids.com/2010/alex-holmes-making-a-stand-from-bullied-to-anti-bullying-leader

bullyingnoway.gov.au

takeastandtogether.gov.au

CYBER-BULLYING

www.kidscape.org.uk/young-people/staying-safe-online

www.stopbullying.gov/cyberbullying

www.thinkuknow.co.uk Child Exploitation and Online Protection Centre (CEOP)

www.youtube.com/user/ceop

DEPRESSION

www.nhs.uk/Conditions/Depression

www.clinical-depression.co.uk

www.blackdogtribe.com Ruby Wax's website and her book: *Sane New World: Taming The Mind*

DIVORCE

www.kidshealth.org go to the teen section and search "Divorce" or, if you want to show your parents, go to the parents section and search "Divorce"

Book: *Divorce helpbook for Teens* by Cynthia Macgregor

DYSLEXIA/DYSPRAXIA

www.bdadyslexia.org.uk British Dyslexia Association

www.dyslexiaaction.org.uk

www.dyslexiascotland.org.uk

www.addressingdyslexia.org Addressing Dyslexia Toolkit (from Dyslexia Scotland but available wherever you are; has a section for parents and one for young people, as well as one for teachers).

www.dyspraxicteens.org.uk/forum

EATING DISORDERS – ANOREXIA AND BULIMIA

www.mentalhealth.org.uk/help-information/mental-health-a-z/E/eating-disorders

www.helpguide.org/mental/anorexia_signs_symptoms_causes_treatment.htm

Remember my advice about avoiding blogs and sites that encourage anorexia. These are sometimes called Pro-Ana or Pro-Anorexia sites. Eating disorders are illnesses that can damage your health long-term and these sites can make you feel much worse in the end.

FORCED MARRIAGE

www.gov.uk/forced-marriage

HEARING VOICES

www.mentalhealth.org.uk/help-information/mental-health-a-z/H/hearing-voices

www.voicecollective.co.uk

www.hearingthevoice.org/looking-for-support

www.intervoiceonline.org and see the section aimed at young people

HYPERHIDROSIS (SWEATING TOO MUCH)

www.hyperhidrosisuk.org

LGBT

www.itgetsbetter.org

teens.webmd.com and search "LGBT"

NEGATIVE THINKING

www.psychcentral.com/lib/2006/about-cognitive-psychotherapy

www.cognitivebiasmodification.com

www.stressbusting.co.uk/cognitive-bias-modification

www.nhs.uk/Conditions/stress-anxiety-depression/Pages/
free-therapy-or-counselling.aspx

OCD

www.kidshealth.org/teen/your_mind/mental_health/ocd.html

www.ocduk.org

www.anxietyuk.org.uk

www.ocfoundation.org Exposure and Response Prevention

Book: *Break Free From OCD: Overcoming Obsessive Compulsive Disorder with CBT* by Dr Fiona Challacombe and others

PREGNANCY

www.brook.org.uk/find-a-centre to find a Brook Centre near you

RAPE

www.kidshealth.org/teen/your_mind/relationships/date_rape.html

www.rapecrisis.org.uk/centres.php
Tel: 0808 802 99 99 England and Wales

www.rapecrisisscotland.org.uk/help/local-centres
Tel: 08088 01 03 02 Scotland

RELATIONSHIPS

**www.kidshealth.org/teen/your_mind/relationships/healthy_
relationship.html** for information about love and sex etc

SELF-HARM

**www.kidshealth.org/teen/your_mind/mental_health/cutting.
html**

www.selfharm.co.uk

Remember to avoid blogs and websites which seem to encourage self-harm or make it seem cool or romantic. These sites can be dangerous. The best help comes from sites run by people who understand that self-harming is a problem and that you need help to stop.

SOCIAL ANXIETY DISORDER / SOCIAL PHOBIA

www.social-anxiety.org.uk

**www.socialanxietydisorder.about.com/od/childrenandsad/tp/
Social-Anxiety-In-Teenagers.htm**

www.nhs.co.uk/conditions/social-anxiety

STEP-FAMILIES

www.careforthefamily.org.uk/stepfamily

STIS /STDs
(Sexually transmitted infections/diseases)

www.brook.org.uk/find-a-centre to find a Brook Centre near you

www.freetest.me for a free Chlamydia test

www.nhs.uk/Livewell/STIs

TRICHOTILLOMANIA

www.trichotillomania.co.uk

YOUNG CARERS

www.barnardos.org.uk scroll to the bottom of the page and select "Young Carers"

www.carers.org

www.carers.org/community/young-adult/blog for a young-adult carers blog

Specific solutions and treatments

CBT
(Cognitive Behavioural Therapy)

www.nhs.uk/Conditions/cognitive-behavioural-therapy

www.psychcentral.com/lib/2006/about-cognitive-psychotherapy

www.ocfoundation.org/cbt.aspx CBT for OCD

COGNITIVE BIAS MODIFICATION

www.cognitivebiasmodification.com

www.stressbusting.co.uk/cognitive-bias-modification

COLOUR THERAPY

www.getselfhelp.co.uk/colour.htm

DIALECTICAL BEHAVIOUR THERAPY

www.getselfhelp.co.uk/dbt.htm

EMDR
(Eye Movement Desensitisation and Reprocessing)

www.emdrassociation.org.uk

www.emdrassociation.org.uk/home/children_and_adolescents.htm

EXPOSURE AND RESPONSE PREVENTION
(For OCD)

www.ocfoundation.org/cbt.aspx

HYPNOTHERAPY

www.thehypnotherapyassociation.co.uk

LAUGHTER

www.helpguide.org/life/humor_laughter_health.htm

www.howstuffworks.com and search for "Laughter"

MINDFULNESS

www.mindfulnessinschools.org

www.mindfulnessinschools.org/resources

Book: *Sane New World: Taming The Mind* by Ruby Wax

NLP
(Neuro-linguistic Programming)

www.nlpkids.co.uk/teens

Book: *Engaging NLP – Teens* by Judy Bartkowiak

www.getselfhelp.co.uk/docs/ImagerySelfHelp.pdf positive imagery and positive visualisation

PSYCHOANALYSIS

www.psychoanalysis.org.uk/clinic/child-services.php

RELAXATION

www.mentalhealth.org.uk/help-information/podcasts free relaxation podcasts

www.innerhealthstudio.com

au.reachout.com/Anxiety-breath

There is a free relaxation audio on my website:
www.nicolamorgan.com

Index

Acknowledgements

I couldn't have done this on my own – imagine the stress levels!
So, I'd like to thank the people who helped:

Sharon Birch, Joanna Cannon, and Damian Wightman, for their expert opinions;
everyone at Walker Books, especially Caz, Alice, Beth,
Hannah, Paul and Molly; my steadfast agent, Elizabeth Roy;
and right-hand woman, Louise Kelly.

For sparking the idea in the first place, all the school librarians
and teachers who invited me to talk about the teenage brain and kept
saying "Can you add something about stress?"

And for being wise, individual, brave, ambitious and just getting
on with life as best they can, my teenage advisers, led by my brilliant niece,
Megan, along with Patrick, Isla, Daryl, Jenni, Kirsty and a group of pupils from the
wonderful Larbert High School in Scotland.

And a special mention to Helen Moss, whose generous bid in the
'Authors for Philippines' fund-raising initiative won her the first signed
copy of this book.

Books by the same author